STATISTICAL LEARNING WITH PYTHON

The Essential Guide for Data-Driven Decisions

Contents

This book utilizes Python, a versatile and beginner-friendly programming language widely used in data analysis and machine learning. No prior coding experience is necessary – we'll guide you step-by-step.

Written by a data science expert with a passion for clear communication, this book equips you with the skills and knowledge to confidently analyze data and translate insights into actionable strategies.

Tired of data overwhelm? This book unveils the secrets to transforming numbers into impactful narratives. Master data analysis techniques, explore data visualization tools, and learn how to craft compelling data stories that drive informed decision-making.

What's Inside?
- Practical hands-on projects to solidify your learning.
- In-depth explanations of essential data analysis concepts.
- Clear and concise code examples using Python libraries like pandas and Matplotlib.
- Ethical considerations for responsible data use.
- Proven storytelling techniques to captivate your audience with data insights.

This book is designed for anyone curious about the power of data analysis, from business professionals to marketing specialists, entrepreneurs, and students. No matter your background, you can unlock the potential of data-driven decision making!

Invest a few hours learning these valuable skills, and reap the rewards of data-driven success for years to come.

Stop feeling lost in a sea of data. Unleash the power of data storytelling! Get your copy today and embark on your journey to becoming a data analysis rockstar.

Table of Contents

Part 1: Foundations for Data-Driven Decisions

Chapter 1: Embracing the Power of Data

Welcome to the exciting world of data-driven decision-making. In this chapter, we'll embark on a journey to understand how statistical learning empowers you to transform raw data into actionable insights.

1.1 The Data Revolution: Unveiling the Hidden Language of Numbers

The world around us is brimming with data. Every click, swipe, purchase, and social media interaction generates a digital footprint. But this vast ocean of information remains silent until we unlock its secrets with the power of statistical learning.

A retail store relying solely on gut instinct to predict customer preferences. They might overstock on unpopular items while missing out on potential best-sellers. Now, consider the same store leveraging statistical learning. By analyzing past sales data, they can identify buying patterns, predict customer demand, and optimize inventory. This is just one glimpse into the transformative power of data-driven decision-making.

Statistical learning equips you with the tools to translate the cryptic language of numbers into actionable insights. Let's dive deeper into how it impacts various aspects of our lives.

1.1.1 From Intuition to Insight: The Rise of Data-Driven Decisions

For centuries, human intuition has guided decision-making. However, intuition can be biased and subjective. Statistical learning offers a more objective approach, relying on concrete evidence from data analysis.

Consider a streaming service struggling with subscriber churn (customers cancelling their subscriptions). Traditionally, they might implement retention strategies based on assumptions about user behavior. Statistical learning empowers them to analyze user data and identify patterns. They might discover that viewers who frequently abandon shows after the first episode are more likely to cancel. Armed with this insight, the streaming service can personalize recommendations and target these users with content they're more likely to engage with, ultimately reducing churn.

This example highlights the shift from intuition-based choices to data-driven insights. Statistical learning provides a framework for uncovering hidden patterns and relationships within data, enabling you to make informed decisions backed by evidence.

1.1.2 Beyond Crystal Balls: Predicting the Future with Data

Wouldn't it be amazing to predict future trends and market behavior? While statistical learning isn't a crystal ball, it offers powerful tools for forecasting.

Let's look at an e-commerce company aiming to optimize their marketing campaigns. By analyzing past sales data and customer demographics, they can identify trends in purchasing behavior. For example, they might discover a surge in demand for summer clothing in the months leading to spring. Using this insight, they can launch targeted marketing campaigns well in advance, maximizing sales and customer satisfaction.

Statistical learning empowers you to move beyond guesswork and anticipate future trends. By analyzing historical data and identifying patterns, you can make informed predictions that contribute to strategic planning and proactive decision-making.

1.1.3 Hands-on with Python: Exploring a Public Dataset

Installing Python and Bash on Different Operating Systems

There are slight variations in the installation process depending on your operating system. Here's a breakdown for the most common ones:

Windows 10/11

Option 1: Using the Official Python Installer

1. Download the latest Python installer from the official website: https://www.python.org/downloads/.

2. Run the downloaded installer. Make sure to check the option to "Add Python 3.x to PATH" during installation. This ensures you can access Python from the command prompt.

3. Open a Command Prompt window (search for "cmd" in the Start menu).

4. Type **`python --version`** and press Enter. If the installation was successful, you'll see the installed Python version displayed.

Option 2: Using Anaconda

Anaconda is a popular Python distribution that comes bundled with various scientific libraries.

1. Download the Anaconda installer from: https://www.anaconda.com/blog/anaconda-individual-edition-2021-11.

2. Run the downloaded installer and follow the on-screen instructions.

3. Open a Command Prompt window.

4. Type **`python --version`** and press Enter. This will show the Python version included in the Anaconda installation.

Bash on Windows:

Since Windows doesn't come with Bash pre-installed, you'll need to enable the Windows Subsystem for Linux (WSL).

1. Search for "Turn Windows features on or off" in the Start menu.

2. Locate "Windows Subsystem for Linux" and check the box next to it.

3. Click "OK" and follow any on-screen instructions to complete the installation.

4. Once WSL is installed, open the Microsoft Store and search for "Linux for Windows". Choose your preferred Linux distribution (e.g., Ubuntu) and install it.

5. Launch the installed Linux distribution. This will open a Bash shell where you can use all the standard Linux commands.

macOS

Python usually comes pre-installed on macOS. Here's how to verify and update if needed:

1. Open a Terminal window (search for "Terminal" in Spotlight).

2. Type **`python3 --version`** and press Enter. If Python is installed, you'll see the version displayed.

3. If Python is not installed or you need to update to a newer version, you can use a package manager like Homebrew. Instructions for installing Homebrew and Python with Homebrew can be found here: https://realpython.com/lessons/installing-python-macos/

Linux Distributions

Most Linux distributions come with Python pre-installed. Here's how to verify and update if needed (commands may vary slightly depending on your distribution):

1. Open a terminal window.

2. Type **python3 --version** and press Enter. This will display the installed Python version.

3. To update Python, use your distribution's package manager. For example, on Ubuntu/Debian, you can use the following command:

Bash

```
sudo apt update && sudo apt upgrade python3
```

Verifying Bash Installation:

- Open a terminal window (Command Prompt on Windows, Terminal on macOS/Linux).

- Type **`echo $SHELL`** and press Enter. If Bash is installed correctly, the output will be something like "/bin/bash".

By following these steps, you should have Python and Bash successfully installed on your system, ready for you to explore the world of data analysis!

Now, let's get started with some real-world data exploration using Python! We'll delve into a publicly available dataset to witness the power of data firsthand.

Here's what we'll be doing:

1. **Importing Libraries:** We'll need the pandas library to manipulate and analyze data. Install it using the following command in your terminal or command prompt:

Bash

```bash
pip install pandas
```

2. **Obtaining the Dataset**: We'll be using the Iris flower dataset, a popular benchmark dataset for machine learning tasks. You can download it directly using the sklearn library:

Python

```python
from sklearn.datasets import load_iris

# Load the Iris flower dataset

iris = load_iris()
```

3. **Examining the Data:** Now, let's peek into the structure of our dataset:

Python

```python
# Print the first few rows of the data

print(iris.data[:5])

# Print the feature names (column names)

print(iris.feature_names)
```

Running this code will display the first few rows of the dataset and reveal the names of the features (e.g., sepal length, sepal width, petal length, petal width).

4. **Visualizing the Data:** Data visualization is crucial for initial exploration. Let's create a scatter plot to explore the relationship between two features:

Python

```python
import matplotlib.pyplot as plt

# Create a scatter plot of sepal length vs sepal width
```

```
plt.scatter(iris.data[:, 0], iris.data[:, 1])    #
Select first two features (sepal length, sepal
width)

plt.xlabel("Sepal length (cm)")

plt.ylabel("Sepal width (cm)")

plt.title("Iris Sepal Length vs Width")

plt.show()
```

This code snippet will generate a scatter plot, allowing you to visually inspect potential relationships between these features.

By working with this dataset, you've taken your first steps into the exciting world of data exploration using Python. As you progress through this book, you'll learn more sophisticated techniques for unlocking the secrets hidden within data

1.2 Unveiling the Data Landscape: Understanding Data Types

Data, data everywhere! But not all data is created equal. In our quest to extract knowledge from information, understanding different data types is crucial. They influence the way we store, analyze, and interpret data using statistical learning techniques. Let's delve into the three fundamental data types you'll encounter frequently:

1.2.1 Numerical Data: The Language of Numbers

In a world where everything is quantified! Numerical data represents information using numbers. It forms the backbone of many statistical analyses. Here are some common examples you might encounter:

- **Sales figures:** The number of units sold for a product.

- **Customer ages:** The age of each customer in a dataset.

- **Website traffic:** The number of visitors to a website on a particular day.

- **Sensor readings:** Temperature readings from a weather station.

When working with numerical data, we can perform various calculations (addition, subtraction, multiplication, etc.) to uncover patterns and trends. For instance, by analyzing sales figures, we might identify which products are most popular or during which months sales peak.

1.2.2 Categorical Data: Sorting the World into Groups

Not everything fits neatly into numbers. Categorical data classifies information into distinct categories. Imagine sorting your socks by color – that's categorical data in action! Here are some examples:

- **Customer preferences:** Preferred brand of clothing (e.g., Brand A, Brand B, Brand C).
- **Customer demographics:** Country of residence (e.g., USA, UK, Canada).
- **Product categories:** Category of a product (e.g., electronics, clothing, furniture).
- **Survey responses:** Responses to a yes/no or multiple-choice question (e.g., Yes, No, Maybe).

While we can't directly perform calculations on categorical data like we do with numbers, it still holds valuable insights. For example, analyzing customer preferences can help businesses understand which brands their customers favor.

1.2.3 Text Data: The Power of Words

The world is full of text – emails, social media posts, customer reviews, and more. This rich source of information falls under text data. While seemingly unstructured, text data can be surprisingly revealing with the right techniques. Here are some examples:

- **Customer reviews:** Feedback from customers about a product or service.
- **Social media comments:** Public opinions and discussions on social media platforms.
- **Email content:** The text of emails sent or received.
- **News articles:** The content of news articles on various topics.

Unlocking the secrets within text data often involves techniques like sentiment analysis, which can determine the overall positive, negative, or neutral sentiment expressed in the text. This can be crucial for understanding customer satisfaction or gauging public opinion on a particular topic.

1.2.4 Working with Data Types in Python

Let's see how to identify data types in Python using the pandas library:

Python

```
import pandas as pd

# Create a sample dataset

data = {
```

```python
    "customer_id": [123, 456, 789],  # Numerical data (unique customer IDs)

    "age": [25, 32, 41],          # Numerical data (customer ages)

    "location": ["New York", "London", "Tokyo"],  # Categorical data (city)

    "review": [

        "This product is amazing!",  # Text data (customer review)

        "Not impressed with the quality.",

        "Great value for the price!"

    ]

}

# Load the data into a pandas DataFrame

df = pd.DataFrame(data)

# Print the data types of each column

print(df.dtypes)
```

This code snippet creates a sample dataset containing various data types. Running the code will display the data types for each column (e.g., int64 for numerical data like customer ID, object for categorical data like location, and object for text data like review).

By understanding data types, you can choose appropriate statistical learning techniques tailored to extract the most valuable insights from your information. Remember, data is like a puzzle – understanding the pieces (data types) is essential to solving the bigger picture!

1.3 Hands-on Project: Unveiling the Secrets of a Public Dataset

Welcome to your first foray into the exciting world of data exploration using Python. In this project, you'll be delving into a publicly available dataset to witness the power of data firsthand. Buckle up, and let's embark on a step-by-step journey:

1. Choosing Your Data Playground:

The world of open data is vast! Numerous websites offer datasets on various topics, from government statistics to social media trends. Here are some popular resources to get you started:

- **Kaggle:** https://www.kaggle.com/datasets

- **UCI Machine Learning Repository:** https://archive.ics.uci.edu/
- **Quandl:** https://data.nasdaq.com/publishers/QDL (economic and financial data)
- **Data.gov:** https://data.gov/ (US government data)

Take some time to browse these websites and choose a dataset that piques your curiosity. It can be something related to your interests, like sports statistics, movie ratings, or weather data. The key is to find a dataset that's publicly available and downloadable.

2. Importing the Cavalry: Pandas to the Rescue!

Once you've chosen your dataset, it's time to import the essential tool for data manipulation – the pandas library. If you haven't already, install it using the following command in your terminal or command prompt:

Bash

```
pip install pandas
```

3. Downloading the Dataset (Specific Instructions will vary):

The method for downloading datasets will vary depending on the website you choose. Here's a general approach:

1. Locate the dataset you want on the website.
2. Look for a download button or option (might be labeled "Download", "CSV Download", or similar).
3. Choose the appropriate file format for your analysis. Common formats include CSV (Comma-Separated Values) or Excel spreadsheets (XLS/XLSX).
4. Download the file and save it in a convenient location on your computer.

Important Note: Always check the website's terms of use or licensing information before downloading any data.

4. Loading the Data into a DataFrame:

Now, let's use pandas to read the downloaded data into a structured format called a DataFrame. Here's an example assuming you downloaded a CSV file named "my_dataset.csv":

Python

```
import pandas as pd
# Replace "my_dataset.csv" with the actual filename of your downloaded data
```

```
data = pd.read_csv("my_dataset.csv")


# Print the first few rows of the data to get a glimpse

print(data.head())


# Print information about the DataFrame, including number of rows and
columns

print(data.info())
```

This code snippet will:

- Import the pandas library.
- Use the pd.read_csv function to read the data from your CSV file.
- Print the first few rows of the data using the head() method. This gives you a preliminary look at the data structure.
- Print information about the DataFrame using the info() method. This reveals details like the number of rows and columns, data types of each column, and presence of any missing values.

5. Exploring the Data Landscape:

With the data loaded, it's time to delve deeper! Here are some key aspects to examine:

- **Column Names:** Identify the names assigned to each column in your DataFrame. These names represent the features or attributes within your data.
- **Data Types:** As discussed earlier, understanding data types (numerical, categorical, text) is crucial for choosing appropriate analysis techniques. Use the dtypes attribute of your DataFrame to see the data type of each column.
- **Missing Values:** Real-world datasets often contain missing values (represented by NaN or null). Use the isna().sum() method to identify the number of missing values within each column. Decide how you'll handle these missing values later in your analysis (e.g., removing rows with missing values, imputing missing values with estimates).

6. Visualizing the Data:

Data visualization is a powerful tool for uncovering patterns and trends. While optional at this stage, you can use libraries like matplotlib or seaborn to create basic plots (histograms, scatter plots) to gain preliminary insights from the data.

This is just the first step on your data exploration journey! By following these steps and exploring the functionalities of pandas, you'll gain the confidence to tackle more complex datasets and extract valuable knowledge using statistical learning techniques

7. Putting it All Together: Example with a Movie Dataset

Let's illustrate the data exploration process with a concrete example. We'll use a movie dataset to showcase the steps involved. Here's how it would look:

1. Choosing the Dataset:

We'll be using the **TMDb movie dataset** available on Kaggle: https://www.kaggle.com/datasets/tmdb/tmdb-movie-metadata This dataset contains information about various movies, including titles, genres, release dates, and ratings.

2. Downloading the Dataset:

1. Visit the link above and click on the "Download" button.
2. Choose the "CSV" format for download.
3. Save the downloaded file as "movies.csv" in your working directory.

3. Loading the Data into a DataFrame:

Python

```python
import pandas as pd

# Read the CSV file into a DataFrame

data = pd.read_csv("movies.csv")

# Print the first 5 rows

print(data.head())


# Get information about the DataFrame

print(data.info())
```

4. Exploring the Data Landscape:

Running the code above will display the first few rows of the data and reveal details like the number of rows, columns, and data types. Let's delve deeper:

- **Column Names:** We see columns like "title," "genre," "release_date," and "vote_average" (average user rating).

- **Data Types:** Some columns are likely objects (text data) like "title" and "genre," while others might be numerical like "release_date" (needs further investigation) and "vote_average."
- **Missing Values:** Use data.isna().sum() to check for missing values. We'll handle these later if needed.

5. Visualization:

Let's create a histogram to visualize the distribution of movie ratings:

Python

```
import matplotlib.pyplot as plt


# Create a histogram of the vote_average column

plt.hist(data["vote_average"])

plt.xlabel("Vote Average")

plt.ylabel("Number of Movies")

plt.title("Distribution of Movie Ratings in the TMDb Dataset")

plt.show()
```

This code will generate a histogram showing the number of movies within each rating range.

There's much more you can explore with this dataset. For instance, you might analyze the relationship between release year and average rating, or identify the most popular genres among highly-rated movies. The possibilities are endless!

Congratulations! You've successfully completed your first hands-on project in data exploration using Python. As you progress through this book, you'll learn more sophisticated techniques for unlocking the hidden stories within data and using them to make informed decisions.

Chapter 2: Building Your Python Toolbox

Welcome, data enthusiasts! Now that you've grasped the power of data and unveiled the secrets of datasets, it's time to equip yourselves with the essential tools for statistical learning. This chapter will introduce you to the wonderful world of Python programming, specifically focusing on the libraries that will become your loyal companions on your data analysis journey.

2.1 Demystifying Python: Your Gateway to Data Exploration

Welcome, aspiring data explorers! Have you ever wondered how seemingly endless streams of information can be transformed into valuable insights? The answer lies in the power of programming, and Python is your friendly guide on this exciting journey.

Here's what makes Python the perfect language for data analysis:

1. Readability Like a Friend: Unlike some programming languages with complex syntax that resemble cryptic messages, Python reads almost like plain English. It's clear and concise structure makes it easier to learn, even for beginners with no prior coding experience. This means less time deciphering code and more time focusing on the fascinating world of data!

2. Instant Gratification (Almost!): Python offers a fantastic feature called an interpreter. This allows you to execute code line by line and see the results immediately. Imagine testing a recipe one step at a time – that's the beauty of the interpreter! It empowers you to experiment, learn from mistakes, and build your confidence as you progress.

3. Powerful Tools at Your Fingertips: While Python itself is not specifically designed for data analysis, it boasts a rich ecosystem of libraries that act as specialized toolkits. These libraries provide a vast array of functions tailored for data manipulation, visualization, and even machine learning – the core ingredients for unlocking the secrets hidden within data.

4. A Language for All Seasons: Python's versatility extends far beyond data analysis. Whether you're interested in web development, creating automated scripts, or even venturing into the realm of artificial intelligence, Python equips you with the skills to tackle various programming challenges. Think of it as a Swiss Army knife for the coding world!

Let's Get Started!

Here's a simple Python program to illustrate its readability and ease of use:

Python

```python
# Print a message to the world

print("Hello, data enthusiasts! Welcome to the
world of Python!")

# Ask the user for their name and store it in a
variable

name = input("What's your name? ")

# Greet the user by name

print(f"It's a pleasure to meet you, {name}!")
```

This short program demonstrates some basic Python concepts:

- **Comments:** Lines starting with "#" are comments and are ignored by the interpreter. These are helpful notes for you or others reading the code.
- **Print function:** The print() function displays messages on the screen.
- **Variables:** Variables like name store data that can be used later in your program.
- **User Input:** The input() function allows users to interact with your program by entering information.

By running this code, you'll see the greeting message displayed, followed by a prompt asking for your name. Once you enter your name and press Enter, the program personalizes the greeting

2.2 Essential Libraries for Statistical Learning:

Now that you've explored the wonders of Python, it's time to meet the all-star players that will transform you from a data novice to a statistical learning whiz! We'll delve into the fantastic three – pandas, NumPy, and scikit-learn – libraries that will become your loyal companions on your data analysis journey.

1. pandas: The Data Wrangler

Imagine a messy room overflowing with unlabeled boxes – that's kind of how raw data can feel. pandas comes to the rescue as your data cleaning and organizing superhero! Here's what it brings to the table:

- **Taming the Beast: Data Structures** – pandas introduces the concept of DataFrames, a powerful data structure that resembles a spreadsheet. Think of it as a labeled table where each row represents a data point (like an item in a box) and each column represents a specific feature or attribute (like the item's name or category). DataFrames make data manipulation and exploration a breeze!

- **Reading and Writing:** pandas can import data from various file formats like CSV, Excel, and even databases, acting as your gateway to the information treasure trove. It also allows you to export your analyzed data for further use or sharing with others.

- **Data Transformation – Shaping Up for Analysis:** pandas offers a vast arsenal of tools to transform your data into the perfect shape for analysis. You can sort data based on specific columns, filter rows that meet certain criteria, or even group similar data points together. Think of it as organizing your messy room – sorting items by category, discarding unnecessary things, and making everything easily accessible for further exploration.

Here's a simple code example to demonstrate creating a DataFrame from a list of dictionaries:

Python

```python
# Sample data representing purchases at a grocery
store

data = [

    {"item": "apple", "price": 1.25, "category":
"fruit"},

    {"item": "milk", "price": 3.50, "category":
"dairy"},

    {"item": "bread", "price": 2.75, "category":
"bakery"}

]


# Import pandas library

import pandas as pd
```

```
# Create a DataFrame from the list

df = pd.DataFrame(data)

# Print the first few rows of the DataFrame (like
peeking into a few boxes)

print(df.head())
```

This code creates a DataFrame named df containing information about grocery items. Running the code will display the first few rows (think peeking into a few boxes), giving you a glimpse of your organized data.

2. NumPy: The Numerical Powerhouse

While pandas excels in data manipulation, NumPy shines in the realm of numerical computations. Imagine a team of super-fast math whizzes – that's essentially what NumPy offers! Here's how it empowers your data analysis:

- **Speedy Calculations:** NumPy utilizes multidimensional arrays for storing and manipulating numerical data. These arrays are like high-performance containers specifically designed for performing calculations on large datasets, making NumPy significantly faster than using standard Python lists for numerical operations.

- **Linear Algebra Magic:** NumPy provides functions for complex mathematical operations like matrix multiplication, which are fundamental building blocks for many machine learning algorithms. Think of it as a magic calculator that can handle even the most challenging equations, making it a valuable tool for tasks like image recognition or recommendation systems.

- **Integration with pandas:** The beauty lies in seamless collaboration! NumPy arrays can be effortlessly converted into pandas DataFrames and vice versa. This smooth data flow between the two libraries allows you to leverage the strengths of each for a more efficient workflow.

Here's a basic example showcasing NumPy arrays:

Python

```python
# Import NumPy library

import numpy as np

# Create a NumPy array containing grocery item
prices

prices = np.array([1.25, 3.50, 2.75])

# Calculate the average price using NumPy
functions

average_price = np.mean(prices)

print("Average price of groceries:", average_price)
```

In this code, we create a NumPy array representing the prices of our grocery items. Then, we use the `np.mean` function to calculate the average price in a single line – that's the power of NumPy's numerical efficiency!

3. scikit-learn: The Machine Learning Arsenal

As you progress through this book, you'll delve into the fascinating world of machine learning, where computers learn from data to make predictions. scikit-learn is your one-stop shop for implementing various machine learning algorithms. Think of it as a vast toolbox containing:

- **Classification Algorithms:** These algorithms allow you to train models to predict categories. Imagine a machine learning model that, after analyzing email content, can classify an email as spam or not spam. scikit-learn provides tools for various classification tasks.

- **Regression Algorithms:** Regression algorithms help you build models to predict continuous values. For instance, you could train a model to predict future housing prices based on features like square footage and location. scikit-learn offers a variety of regression techniques for different prediction scenarios.

- **Clustering Algorithms:** Clustering algorithms group similar data points together, helping you identify hidden patterns within your data. Imagine grouping customers with similar buying habits to create targeted marketing campaigns. scikit-learn provides various clustering algorithms to uncover these hidden relationships.

- **Model Evaluation:** Once you've trained a machine learning model, you need to assess its performance. scikit-learn offers metrics and tools to evaluate how well your model generalizes to unseen data. Think of it as giving your model a final exam to ensure it can perform well on new information.

Installing the Libraries:

Before embarking on your data analysis journey, you'll need to equip yourself with these essential libraries. Open your terminal or command prompt and run the following command:

Bash

```
pip install pandas numpy scikit-learn
```

The Dream Team in Action!

While we haven't delved into the specifics of using these libraries yet (that's coming up in later chapters!), imagine this scenario:

1. You use pandas to import a dataset containing customer information and purchase history.
2. You leverage NumPy to perform calculations on numerical features like purchase amount.
3. You utilize scikit-learn to train a machine learning model that predicts which customers are likely to make repeat purchases.

This is just a glimpse of the power these libraries hold when combined. As you explore further, you'll witness how pandas, NumPy, and scikit-learn work together seamlessly to transform raw data into actionable insights!

2.3 Data Wrangling in Action: Cleaning and Pre-processing Techniques

The road to data analysis is paved with good intentions... and clean data! In the real world, datasets often come with imperfections that can hinder your analysis. Missing values, inconsistencies, and formatting errors – these are the unwanted gremlins lurking in your data. Fear not, for data wrangling techniques are here to save the day!

Data wrangling encompasses the essential tasks of cleaning and pre-processing your data to prepare it for analysis. Think of it as tidying up your workspace before diving into a project. Here are some of the common gremlins you'll encounter and how to wrangle them:

1. Identifying Missing Values

Missing data points (often represented by NaN or null values) can disrupt your analysis. Luckily, pandas offers handy tools to identify these troublemakers. The `isna().sum()` function is your secret weapon:

Python

```python
# Import pandas library
import pandas as pd
# Sample data with missing values
data = {'name': ['Alice', None, 'Bob', 'Charlie'], 'age': [25, None, 30, 28]}
df = pd.DataFrame(data)
```

```
# Check for missing values using isna().sum()

print(df.isna().sum())
```

This code creates a DataFrame with a missing name and age value (represented by None). Running the code displays a Series indicating how many missing values exist in each column. Now you know where to focus your cleaning efforts!

2. Handling Missing Values

There's no one-size-fits-all solution for missing data. The best approach depends on the context and the amount of missing data:

- **Dropping Rows/Columns:** If a row or column has too many missing values, it might be best to remove them entirely. Use the `dropna()` function with the appropriate parameters to achieve this.
- **Imputation:** This strategy involves filling in missing values with estimates based on other data points. For instance, you could fill in missing salary data with the average salary in the same job category. pandas offers functions like `fillna()` for imputation techniques.

3. Dealing with Outliers

Outliers are data points that fall significantly outside the typical range. While they can sometimes be valuable insights, they can also skew your analysis results. Here's how to handle them:

- **Identifying Outliers:** Use statistical methods like calculating interquartile range (IQR) to identify potential outliers. Libraries like NumPy offer functions for IQR calculations.

- **Winsorization:** This technique replaces outliers with values closer to the rest of the data, capping their influence on analysis. There are libraries like SciPy that provide functions for winsorization.

- **Removal (with Caution):** If outliers are truly erroneous, you might consider removing them. However, proceed with caution as you might be discarding valuable insights.

4. Inconsistency Wrangling

Data inconsistencies can come in various forms – misspelled words, mixed data formats (uppercase/lowercase letters), or incorrect punctuation. pandas offers string manipulation methods to tackle these:

- `str.lower()` **or** `str.upper()`: These functions convert all strings in a column to lowercase or uppercase, ensuring consistency for comparisons.
- `str.strip()`: This function removes leading and trailing whitespaces from strings, ensuring clean comparisons.
- **Regular expressions:** For more complex cleaning tasks, regular expressions provide a powerful tool for searching and manipulating text data. While they have a steeper learning curve, they can be very effective for specific cleaning needs.

Data wrangling is an iterative process. As you explore your data further, you might discover additional cleaning needs. The key is to be attentive to detail and ensure your data is in pristine condition before diving into analysis.

Here's an example (building on the previous code) demonstrating how to handle

missing values by removing rows with missing data:

Python

```
# Drop rows with missing values (be cautious of
data loss!)

df_cleaned = df.dropna()
```

```
# Print the cleaned DataFrame

print(df_cleaned)
```

This code removes any rows containing missing values, resulting in a cleaner DataFrame (but also potentially losing some data). This is just a starting point – there are many other wrangling techniques you'll encounter as you progress in your data analysis journey!

5. Categorical Data Wrangling

Many datasets contain categorical features – data that represent types or classifications rather than numerical values (e.g., hair color, job title). Here's how to handle them:

- **Label Encoding:** This technique assigns numerical labels (like 0, 1, 2) to each category. While seemingly simpler, it can introduce misleading assumptions about the order or relationship between categories (e.g., 2 isn't necessarily "better" than 1).
- **One-Hot Encoding:** This approach creates a new binary column for each category. If a data point belongs to that

category, the corresponding column value is set to 1, otherwise it's 0. This method preserves the categorical nature of the data and is often preferred for machine learning algorithms. Pandas offers the get_dummies() function for one-hot encoding.

6. Feature Scaling

Many machine learning algorithms perform better when features are on a similar scale. Feature scaling techniques like standardization (scaling features to have a mean of 0 and standard deviation of 1) or normalization (scaling features to a specific range like 0 to 1) can address this. Scikit-learn provides functions for various scaling techniques.

The Importance of Data Quality

Remember, data wrangling is an investment in the quality of your analysis. Clean and pre-processed data leads to more reliable results and more accurate insights. As you gain experience, you'll develop a keen eye for identifying data quality issues and become a data wrangling pro!

Hands-on Project: Taming a Messy Dataset

Now, let's put your newfound data wrangling skills to the test! Imagine you're analyzing a dataset containing information about car sales. The data might have missing values, inconsistent formatting, and categorical features that need encoding.

Here's a possible approach (remember, this is just a starting point, and the specific steps might vary depending on the actual data):

1. **Import libraries:** Import pandas and any other libraries you might need for specific cleaning tasks (e.g., SciPy for outlier handling).

2. **Load the data:** Use `pd.read_csv()` to read the car sales data from a CSV file.

3. **Explore the data:** Get a general overview of the data using techniques like `head()`, `describe()`, and `info()`. This helps identify potential issues like missing values or data type inconsistencies.

4. **Handle missing values:** Use `isna().sum()` to identify missing values and decide on an appropriate strategy (dropping

rows,   imputation   techniques).

5. **Clean categorical data:** Identify categorical features and choose an encoding method (label encoding or one-hot encoding) based on your analysis goals. Use pandas' `get_dummies()` function for one-hot encoding, if applicable.

6. **Address inconsistencies:** Use string manipulation methods like `str.lower()`, `str.strip()`, or regular expressions to ensure consistent formatting and data types.

7. **Feature scaling (optional):** If you plan to use machine learning algorithms, consider scaling numerical features using techniques like standardization or normalization from scikit-learn.

8. **Save the cleaned data:** After all the wrangling, save the cleaned DataFrame to a new CSV file for further analysis.

Data wrangling is an iterative process. As you explore your data further, you might discover additional cleaning needs. The key takeaway is to be attentive to detail and ensure your data is in top shape before drawing conclusions.

By mastering data wrangling techniques, you'll transform raw, messy data into a valuable asset for your data analysis journey. This paves the way for exciting explorations in the world of statistical learning, where you'll uncover hidden patterns and make data-driven decisions with confidence!

Hands-on Project 2: Taming a Messy Movie Dataset

Welcome, data wranglers! Now that you're equipped with essential data cleaning and pre-processing techniques, let's roll up our sleeves and tackle a real-world scenario. We'll be working with a movie dataset, but remember, this approach can be applied to various data types!

The Dataset:

For this project, we'll use a dataset containing information about movies, including titles, genres, release years, and potentially some inconsistencies and missing values. This dataset is publicly available online, and you can find it at https://archive.org/details/movies.

Once you've downloaded the file, save it in the same directory as your Python script.

The Objective:

Your mission is to clean and pre-process this movie data using your newfound data wrangling skills! We'll guide you through each step, providing code examples along the way. The goal is to transform this raw data into a well-structured format, ready for further analysis (like exploring popular genres across different decades).

Step 1: Import Libraries and Load Data

1. Open your favorite Python IDE or code editor and create a new Python script.
2. Import the pandas library for data manipulation:

Python

```
import pandas as pd
```

3. Load the movie data from the CSV file using `pd.read_csv()`:

Python

```python
# Replace 'movies.csv' with the actual filename if
it differs
movie_data = pd.read_csv('movies.csv')
```

Step 2: Explore the Data

Before diving into cleaning, get a general sense of what you're working with:

Python

```python
# Get a glimpse of the first few rows
print(movie_data.head())


# View basic summary statistics for numerical
columns
print(movie_data.describe())


# Check for information about data types and
potential missing values
print(movie_data.info())
```

Running this code will display the first few rows of the data, summary statistics (like average release year if present), and information about data types and missing values. This initial exploration helps identify areas that might require cleaning.

Step 3: Handling Missing Values

Use the `isna().sum()` function to identify columns with missing values and decide on an appropriate strategy:

Python

```
# Check for missing values
print(movie_data.isna().sum())
```

Depending on the context and the amount of missing data, you might choose to:

- **Drop rows/columns:** If a row or column has too many missing values, consider removing them using `dropna()`. However, use this approach cautiously to avoid losing valuable data.

- **Imputation:** For specific columns and strategically, you could impute missing values with estimates based on other data points (e.g., filling in missing release year based on the average release year for similar genres). pandas offers functions like `fillna()` for this purpose, but proceed with caution to avoid biasing your data.

Step 4: Cleaning Categorical Data (Genres)

The genre information might be a comma-separated list (e.g., "Comedy, Drama"). We'll need to transform this into a more usable format for analysis. Here are two options:

- **Splitting Genres into Separate Columns:** Use string manipulation techniques like `split()` to create a separate column for each genre within a movie.

Python

```
# Example (assuming 'genre' is the column
containing genre information)
movie_data['genre1']                          =
movie_data['genre'].str.split(',').str[0]
```

```
movie_data['genre2']              (optional)          =
movie_data['genre'].str.split(',').str[1]    # Add
more columns if needed
```

- **One-Hot Encoding (Optional):** This approach creates a new binary column for each unique genre. If a movie belongs to that genre, the corresponding column value is set to 1, otherwise it's 0. Pandas offers the `get_dummies()` function for one-hot encoding, which can be particularly useful for machine learning tasks.

Step 5: Addressing Inconsistencies

Data inconsistencies can come in various forms: misspelled words, mixed uppercase/lowercase letters, or extra spaces. Use string manipulation methods like:

- `str.lower()`: Converts all characters in a column to lowercase for consistent comparisons.
- `str.strip()`: Removes leading and trailing whitespaces from strings.
- Regular expressions (more advanced): For complex cleaning tasks, regular expressions provide a powerful tool for searching and manipulating text data.

Step 6: Feature Scaling

This step is particularly relevant if you plan to use the cleaned movie data for machine learning tasks. Many machine learning algorithms perform better when features are on a similar scale. Techniques like standardization (scaling features to have a mean of 0 and standard deviation of 1) or normalization (scaling features to a specific range like 0 to 1) can address this. Scikit-learn provides functions for various scaling techniques, but for this project focusing on data wrangling, we'll skip this step for now.

Step 7: Save the Cleaned Data

After all your hard work, it's time to save the wrangled data for future analysis! Use `to_csv()` to export your cleaned DataFrame to a new CSV file:

Python

```python
# Save the cleaned data to a new CSV file
movie_data.to_csv('cleaned_movies.csv',
index=False)   # Avoid saving the index column

print("Data cleaning complete! Your wrangled movie
data is saved as 'cleaned_movies.csv'")
```

Data wrangling is an iterative process. As you explore your data further, you might discover additional cleaning needs. The key takeaway is to be attentive to detail and ensure your data is in pristine condition before drawing conclusions.

You've successfully completed your first data wrangling project! By following these steps and using the provided code examples, you've transformed a messy movie dataset into a well-structured format, ready for further exploration. This is a valuable skill that will empower you to tackle various data analysis challenges in the future.

Chapter 3: Unveiling the Landscape of Statistical Learning

Welcome, intrepid data explorers! As you embark on your journey into statistical learning, this chapter serves as your roadmap. We'll unveil core concepts, explore different learning algorithms, and equip you with tools to evaluate their performance. Buckle up, and get ready to unlock the secrets hidden within your data!

3.1 Core Concepts: Supervised vs. Unsupervised Learning

Welcome to the fascinating world of statistical learning! This chapter lays the foundation for your journey by exploring two fundamental approaches: supervised and unsupervised learning. Think of them as different paths to uncover the secrets hidden within your data.

Supervised Learning: Learning with a Teacher

Imagine you're presented with a box of jumbled toys – balls, cars, dolls – all mixed together. Supervised learning is like having a helpful friend who sorts the toys into labeled categories (balls, cars, dolls). This friend acts as your **teacher**, providing **labeled examples**. The statistical learning algorithm then observes these labeled examples and learns to identify patterns that map the inputs (toys) to their corresponding labels (categories).

Here's a breakdown of the key aspects of supervised learning:

- **Labeled Data:** The core concept is the presence of labeled data. Each data point has a predefined label or output value that you want the model to predict. In our toy analogy, the labels are the categories (ball, car, doll).

- **Learning from Examples:** The algorithm learns by analyzing the labeled data. It's like studying the sorting done by your friend and understanding the characteristics that differentiate balls from cars.

- **Prediction on New Data:** Once trained, the model can predict labels for new, unseen data. Presented with an unlabeled toy (a new data point), the model can use its learned knowledge to classify it as a ball, car, or doll (predicting the label).

Common Supervised Learning Tasks:

- **Regression:** This involves predicting continuous values. For instance, a supervised learning model could be trained on data points containing house prices (labels) and features like square footage and location. The model could then predict the price of a new house based on its features.

- **Classification:** Here, the goal is to categorize data points into predefined classes. Imagine training a model on labeled emails (spam or not spam) and then using it to classify new incoming emails.

Supervised Learning Algorithms:

There's a whole toolbox of supervised learning algorithms, each with its strengths and applications. We'll explore some of these in more detail later in the chapter.

Unsupervised Learning: Discovery Without Labels

Now, imagine you're presented with a box containing unrecognizable objects – unlike the labeled toys. This is where unsupervised learning comes in. Unlike supervised learning, it deals with **unlabeled data**. The algorithm ventures into uncharted territory, seeking to identify hidden patterns or structures within the data itself. It's like exploring a new world and making sense of what you find without a map or predefined categories.

Here are the key characteristics of unsupervised learning:

- **Unlabeled Data:** The data lacks predefined labels or categories. The algorithm doesn't have a teacher telling it what to look for.

- **Uncovering Hidden Patterns:** The unsupervised learning algorithm analyzes the data to discover inherent groupings, patterns, or relationships. Imagine finding clusters of similar objects within the box, even though you don't have predefined categories like "toys" or "tools."

- **Dimensionality Reduction (Optional):** In some cases, unsupervised learning techniques can help reduce the number of features (dimensions) in a dataset while preserving essential information. This can be useful for visualization and improving the efficiency of certain algorithms.

Common Unsupervised Learning Tasks:

- **Clustering:** This technique groups similar data points together. Imagine grouping the objects in the box based on their characteristics, even if you don't have predefined labels for those groups.

- **Dimensionality Reduction:** As mentioned earlier, this process reduces the number of features in a dataset while aiming to maintain the most important information. Think of it as simplifying a complex map while preserving the key landmarks for easier navigation.

Choosing the Right Approach:

The choice between supervised and unsupervised learning depends on your data and your goals. Here's a quick rule of thumb:

- Use supervised learning if you have labeled data and want to make predictions (e.g., predicting house prices or classifying emails).
- Use unsupervised learning if your data is unlabeled and you want to explore it to discover hidden patterns or groupings (e.g., understanding customer behavior or segmenting users based on their browsing habits).

By understanding these core concepts, you've taken the first step on your statistical learning journey! In the next sections, we'll delve deeper into specific algorithms and how to evaluate their performance.

3.2 Introduction to Common Statistical Learning Algorithms

Now that you've grasped the fundamental differences between supervised and unsupervised learning, it's time to meet some of the workhorse algorithms that power these approaches! Think of them as the tools in your statistical learning toolbox, each with its strengths and applications.

Supervised Learning Algorithms:

1. **Linear Regression:**
   - **The Straightforward Predictor:** Imagine a straight line that best fits a scatter plot of data points. This line represents the linear relationship between a dependent variable (what you want to predict) and one or more independent variables (features influencing the prediction). Linear regression excels at modeling this linear relationship, allowing you to estimate missing values or make predictions for new data points.

- **Example:** Predicting house prices based on features like square footage and location.

- **Not suitable for:** Highly non-linear relationships between features and target variable.

2. **Logistic Regression:**

   - **Taming the Classification Challenge:** While linear regression tackles continuous values, logistic regression ventures into classification – the world of sorting data points into distinct categories. Imagine a sigmoid function (S-shaped curve) that transforms its input into a probability between 0 and 1. Logistic regression uses this function to model the probability of an event belonging to a specific class (e.g., predicting the probability of an email being spam).

   - **Example:** Classifying emails as spam or not spam.

   - **Not suitable for:** Multi-class classification problems (more than two categories).

3. **Decision Trees:**

  ○ **Learning by Asking Questions:** Imagine a flowchart-like structure that splits the data based on a series of yes/no questions (decision rules). Decision trees follow this approach, recursively dividing the data into smaller and purer subsets until they arrive at a final decision or prediction. Think of a series of questions that lead you to a specific classification (e.g., "Is the email from an unknown sender? Yes -> Is there an attachment? Yes -> Classify as spam").

  ○ **Example:** Classifying customers based on their purchase history for targeted marketing campaigns.

  ○ **Not suitable for:** Very high-dimensional data (many features) as it can lead to overfitting.

4. **K-Nearest Neighbors (KNN):**

- **Learning by Proximity:** This approach leverages the wisdom of the crowd – the k nearest neighbors in the training data – to classify new data points. Imagine finding the k closest data points (based on similarity measures) to a new, unseen data point and assigning the majority class label from those neighbors. KNN essentially relies on the principle that similar data points belong to the same class.

- **Example:** Recommending products to users based on their browsing history and the preferences of similar users.

- **Not suitable for:** High-dimensional data, as distance calculations can become less meaningful. Additionally, KNN can be computationally expensive for large datasets.

5. **Support Vector Machines (SVMs):**

   - **Finding the Optimal Separation:** SVMs aim to create a clear dividing line (or hyperplane in higher dimensions) that best separates data points belonging to different classes. Imagine drawing a line (or a higher-dimensional plane) that maximizes the margin between the two classes, allowing for more accurate classification. SVMs are powerful for classification tasks, particularly when dealing with high-dimensional data.

- **Example:** Classifying handwritten digits (0, 1, 2, etc.) based on pixel information.

- **Not suitable for:** Highly non-linear data, as SVMs work best with linearly separable data (or data that can be transformed to be linearly separable).

This is just a starting point! There are many other supervised learning algorithms available, each with its own advantages and limitations. As you progress in your learning journey, you'll discover more specialized techniques tailored for specific tasks.

The choice of algorithm depends on your data, the nature of your problem (regression or classification), and the desired outcome. Experimentation and evaluation are crucial to finding the best model for your specific needs.

3.3 Understanding Evaluation Metrics:

So you've trained your statistical learning model – congratulations! But before unleashing it on the world (or at least your next dataset), how do you know how well it performs? This is where evaluation metrics come in – the gauges on your statistical learning dashboard. They provide a quantitative measure of how closely your model's predictions align with the actual outcomes.

Choosing the Right Metric:

The choice of metric depends on the type of learning task you're tackling:

- **Regression Problems:** Here, you're predicting continuous values (like house prices or sales figures). Common metrics for regression include:

  - **Mean Squared Error (MSE):** This metric measures the average squared difference between the predicted values and the actual values. Lower MSE indicates better performance, as it signifies that the predictions are, on average, closer to the actual values.

- **Root Mean Squared Error (RMSE):** The RMSE is simply the square root of the MSE. It's often preferred because it's expressed in the same units as the target variable, making it easier to interpret. For instance, an RMSE of $10,000 for a house price prediction model suggests that the predictions are typically off by an average of $10,000.

Here's an example of calculating MSE using Python's numpy library:

Python

```python
import numpy as np
# Sample predicted values and actual values
predicted_values = [10, 15, 8, 12, 11]
actual_values = [8, 12, 10, 14, 12]


# Calculate squared errors
squared_errors = [(p - a)**2 for p, a in zip(predicted_values, actual_values)]


# Calculate mean squared error
mse = np.mean(squared_errors)
```

```
print(f"Mean Squared Error (MSE): {mse}")
```

- **Classification Problems:** In classification, you're assigning data points to predefined categories (like spam or not spam). Here are some key metrics:

  - **Accuracy:** This metric simply calculates the percentage of predictions that were correct. While seemingly straightforward, accuracy can be misleading, especially for imbalanced datasets (where one class has significantly more data points than others).

  - **Precision:** This metric focuses on the positive predictions – out of all the data points your model classified as positive (e.g., spam), how many were actually positive? A high precision indicates that your model is good at identifying true positives and not making many false positive errors.

  - **Recall:** This metric tells you a different story – out of all the actual positive cases in your data, how many did your model correctly identify? A high recall indicates that your model is capturing most of the true positives and not missing many.

- ○ **F1-Score:** This metric combines precision and recall into a single score, providing a balanced view of your model's performance. An F1-score of 1 represents perfect prediction, while a score of 0 indicates the model always predicts the wrong class.

Confusion Matrix:

A confusion matrix is a visualization tool that helps you understand the performance of your classification model across different classes. It shows how many data points from each actual class were predicted into each class by the model. This can reveal issues like high false positives or missed classifications for specific classes.

Beyond the Basics:

These are just some of the core evaluation metrics for regression and classification tasks. As you delve deeper into statistical learning, you'll encounter more specialized metrics tailored to specific algorithms or applications. Additionally, techniques like cross-validation help ensure your evaluation metrics are reliable and generalizable beyond the training data.

Evaluation metrics are essential for guiding your model selection and improvement process. By understanding these metrics and how to interpret them, you can make informed decisions about the performance of your statistical learning models.

Hands-on Project: Unveiling Your Data with Visualization

Congratulations! You've grasped the fundamentals of statistical learning and evaluation metrics. Now, let's dive into the world of data visualization – a crucial skill for exploring your data and uncovering hidden patterns. We'll leverage the power of Python libraries like `matplotlib` and `seaborn` to create informative and visually appealing plots.

Why Visualize Data?

Data visualization serves multiple purposes:

- **Uncover Patterns and Trends:** Visualizations can reveal hidden relationships between variables that might be missed by simply looking at raw numbers. For instance, a scatter plot might show a linear trend between income and education levels.

- **Identify Outliers:** Visualization techniques like boxplots can help you identify data points that fall outside the expected range, which could warrant further investigation.

- **Communicate Insights:** Effective data visualizations can communicate complex information clearly and concisely to both technical and non-technical audiences.

The Tools of the Trade:

- **Matplotlib:** This fundamental Python library provides a versatile toolkit for creating various plots like scatter plots, line plots, and histograms.

- **Seaborn:** Built on top of matplotlib, seaborn offers a high-level interface for creating statistical graphics with a focus on aesthetics and ease of use. It provides pre-defined styles and color schemes, making it simpler to create visually appealing plots.

Getting Started:

1. **Import Libraries:** Begin by importing the necessary libraries:

Python

```python
import pandas as pd

import matplotlib.pyplot as plt

import seaborn as sns
```

2. **Load Your Data:** Use pandas to load your data from a CSV file:

Python

```python
# Replace 'your_data.csv' with the actual filename

data = pd.read_csv('your_data.csv')
```

Exploring Data Distributions:

- **Histograms:** Use histograms to visualize the distribution of a single numerical variable. This helps you understand how the data is spread out and identify potential skewness (lopsidedness).

Python

```python
# Example: Distribution of income levels
sns.histplot(data['income'])    # Replace 'income'
with your column name
plt.xlabel('Income')
plt.ylabel('Number of People')
plt.title('Distribution of Income in the Dataset')
plt.show()
```

- **Boxplots:** Boxplots provide a summary of a numerical variable's distribution, including the median, quartiles (25th and 75th percentiles), and potential outliers.

Python

```python
# Example: Distribution of age across different
genders
sns.boxplot(
    x = 'gender',   # Replace 'gender' with your
categorical column name
    y = 'age',    # Replace 'age' with your
numerical column name
    showmeans=True,  # Display the mean as well
    data=data
)
plt.xlabel('Gender')
plt.ylabel('Age')
plt.title('Distribution of Age by Gender')
plt.show()
```

Visualizing Relationships:

- **Scatter Plots:** Scatter plots show the relationship between two continuous variables. They can reveal linear or non-linear trends, as well as potential clusters or outliers.

Python

```python
# Example: Relationship between experience and salary
sns.scatterplot(
    x = 'experience',  # Replace 'experience' with your column name
    y = 'salary',  # Replace 'salary' with your column name
    data=data
)
plt.xlabel('Years of Experience')
plt.ylabel('Salary')
plt.title('Relationship Between Experience and Salary')
plt.show()
```

- **Heatmaps:** Heatmaps are useful for visualizing relationships between two categorical variables. The intensity of the color in each cell represents the frequency or strength of the association between the categories.

Python

```python
# Example: Correlation between features (assuming numerical features)
```

```
correlation_matrix = data.corr()    # Calculate
correlation matrix
sns.heatmap(correlation_matrix,    annot=True)       #
Display values in each cell
plt.title('Correlation Matrix of Features')
plt.show()
```

These are just a few examples to get you started. Matplotlib and seaborn offer a wide range of plotting functionalities. Explore the documentation and experiment with different visualization techniques to find the ones that best suit your data and analysis goals. Data visualization is an iterative process. As you explore your data and uncover new insights, you might refine your visualizations to better communicate your findings. Effective visualizations not only showcase the data but also tell a clear and compelling story.

Part 2: Mastering Essential Techniques

Chapter 4: Conquering the World of Regression Analysis

Welcome, intrepid data explorers! In this chapter, we delve into the realm of regression analysis, a fundamental technique for modeling relationships between variables. Buckle up and get ready to unlock the secrets of predicting continuous outcomes using the power of statistics!

4.1 Exploring Linear Regression and its Assumptions

Welcome to the fascinating world of regression analysis! This chapter focuses specifically on linear regression, a technique used to model and understand the relationship between a **continuous dependent variable** (what you want to predict) and one or more **independent variables** (factors influencing the prediction). Think of it as a detective story – you're investigating how changes in one variable cause the other to change in a predictable way.

Linear regression excels at uncovering **linear** relationships. Imagine plotting the independent variable on the x-axis and the dependent variable on the y-axis. If the data points roughly follow a straight line, then linear regression might be a good fit for your analysis.

But before you jump right in, there are some key assumptions to consider:

1. **Linear Relationship:** This is the foundation – the core assumption is that the relationship between the independent and dependent variables is indeed linear. In other words, the data points should cluster around a straight line, not a curve or some other more complex shape.

2. **Homoscedasticity:** This tongue-twister simply means the errors (the difference between predicted and actual values) should have a consistent spread (variance) across all levels of the independent variable. Imagine a cloud of data points around the regression line. In an ideal scenario, this cloud should have a constant width, regardless of the independent variable's value.

3. **Normality of Errors:** The errors (also called residuals) in your model are assumed to follow a normal distribution (bell-shaped curve). This ensures the validity of statistical tests used to evaluate the model's performance.

4. **Independence of Errors:** The errors for each data point should be independent of each other. There shouldn't be any correlation or pattern in how the errors vary across your data. In simpler terms, the error for one data point shouldn't influence the error for another.

Vices and Virtues: Violations and Diagnostics

While these assumptions are crucial for interpreting the results of linear regression accurately, real-world data can be messy and may not always perfectly adhere to them. But don't fret! There are techniques to address potential violations, and even if the assumptions aren't perfectly met, linear regression can still provide valuable insights.

Here's a quick trick to remember the assumptions: **L NH I** (Linearity, Homoscedasticity, Normality of Errors, Independence). As you gain experience, you'll develop a toolbox of diagnostic plots and tests to check for these assumptions and identify potential issues.

Code Example: Visualizing Assumptions (Optional):

Here's a basic example using Python's pandas and matplotlib libraries to get you started with visualizing one assumption –

homoscedasticity. This code snippet plots the residuals against the fitted values:

Python

```python
import pandas as pd

import matplotlib.pyplot as plt


# Load your data and fit a linear regression model
(replace with your code)


# Calculate residuals

residuals = y_test - y_predicted


# Scatter plot of residuals vs fitted values

plt.scatter(model.predict(X_test), residuals)

plt.xlabel('Fitted Values')

plt.ylabel('Residuals')

plt.title('Residuals vs Fitted Values')
```

```
plt.show()
```

By looking at this plot, you can see if the spread of the residuals appears consistent across the range of fitted values. If the plot reveals a pattern or increasing/decreasing spread, it might indicate a violation of homoscedasticity.

This is just a glimpse into the world of linear regression assumptions. As you progress, you'll delve deeper into diagnosing violations and exploring techniques to handle them. But for now, keep these core assumptions in mind as you embark on your linear regression journey!

4.2 Implementing Linear Regression with Python (scikit-learn)

Now that you've grasped the fundamentals of linear regression and its assumptions, let's dive into the practical world of implementing a model using Python's `scikit-learn` library! Get ready to transform your data into a prediction machine.

The Step-by-Step Guide:

1. **Import the Necessary Libraries:**

Python

```
import pandas as pd
from        sklearn.model_selection        import
train_test_split
from sklearn.linear_model import LinearRegression
```

- ○ pandas: This library is your workhorse for data manipulation and analysis in Python.
- ○ train_test_split from sklearn.model_selection: This function helps you split your data into training and testing sets, a crucial step for model evaluation.
- ○ LinearRegression from sklearn.linear_model: This class from scikit-learn is what you'll use to create and train your linear regression model.

2. **Load and Prepare Your Data:** Load your data from a CSV file using pandas read_csv function (replace 'your_data.csv' with your actual filename):

Python

```
data = pd.read_csv('your_data.csv')
```

- Identify the features (independent variables) and the target variable (dependent variable) you want to predict.

- Handle missing values (if any) using appropriate techniques like imputation or deletion (depending on your data and analysis goals).

3. **Splitting the Data into Training and Testing Sets:** Use `train_test_split` to split your data into two sets:

Python

```
X_train, X_test, y_train, y_test =
train_test_split(
    data[independent_variables],
data[dependent_variable], test_size=0.2)
```

- **X_train**: This contains the features you'll use to train the model.
- **X_test**: This holds the unseen data points used for testing the model's performance.
- **y_train**: This contains the target values for the training data.
- **y_test**: These are the actual target values for the testing data, used to compare against the model's predictions.
  - The `test_size` parameter specifies the proportion of data allocated to the testing set (e.g., 0.2 for 20%). This ensures the model is evaluated on data it hasn't seen during training.

4. **Creating and Fitting the Model:** Instantiate `LinearRegression` object:

Python

```python
model = LinearRegression()
```

Train the model using the `fit` method. This involves the model learning the coefficients of the linear equation that best represents the relationship between the features and the target variable:

Python

```
model.fit(X_train, y_train)
```

By fitting the model, you essentially teach it the patterns within the training data.

5. **Making Predictions:** Once trained, you can use the model to predict the target variable for new data points. Use the `predict` method:

Python

```
y_predicted = model.predict(X_test)
```

- **y_predicted**: This contains the model's predictions for the target variable on the testing data.

Beyond the Basics:

This code snippet provides a basic framework for linear regression with scikit-learn. As you explore further, you'll encounter more advanced functionalities:

- **Model Evaluation:** We'll delve into techniques like mean squared error (MSE) and root mean squared error (RMSE) to assess how well your model performs on unseen data.

- **Model Interpretation:** By analyzing the coefficients of the fitted model, you can gain insights into the direction and strength of the relationships between the features and the target variable.

- **Feature Selection:** Techniques like LASSO regression can help identify the most important features for your prediction task.

- **Model Regularization:** Regularization methods can help prevent overfitting and improve the model's generalizability to unseen   data.

Remember: This is just the beginning of your linear regression journey with Python. So, experiment with different datasets, explore the extended functionalities of scikit-learn, and get ready to unlock the power of linear regression for your data analysis endeavors!

4.3 Evaluating Model Performance and Diagnosing Issues in Linear Regression

You've trained your linear regression model – congratulations! But before unleashing it on the world (or at least your next dataset), how do you know how well it performs? Here's where evaluation metrics come in – the gauges on your linear regression dashboard. They provide a quantitative measure of how closely your model's predictions align with the actual outcomes.

Choosing the Right Metric:

The choice of metric depends on the nature of your prediction task:

- **Mean Squared Error (MSE):** This metric is a common choice for evaluating the performance of regression models. It measures the average squared difference between the predicted values and the actual values. Lower MSE indicates better performance, as it signifies that the predictions are, on average, closer to the actual values.

Here's how to calculate MSE using Python's numpy library:

Python

```
import numpy as np

# Replace with your predicted and actual values
y_predicted = [10, 15, 8, 12, 11]
y_actual = [8, 12, 10, 14, 12]

# Calculate squared errors
squared_errors  =  [(p  -  a)**2  for  p,  a  in
zip(y_predicted, y_actual)]

# Calculate mean squared error
mse = np.mean(squared_errors)
```

```python
print(f"Mean Squared Error (MSE): {mse}")
```

- **Root Mean Squared Error (RMSE):** The RMSE is simply the square root of the MSE. It's often preferred because it's expressed in the same units as the target variable, making it easier to interpret. For instance, an RMSE of $10,000 for a house price prediction model suggests that the predictions are typically off by an average of $10,000.

Visualizing Model Performance:

- **Scatter Plots:** A scatter plot of the predicted values vs. the actual values can reveal patterns and potential issues. Ideally, the data points should cluster around a diagonal line, indicating that the predictions are closely aligned with the actual values.

Python

```python
import matplotlib.pyplot as plt

plt.scatter(y_test, y_predicted)    # Replace with
your test data
plt.xlabel('Actual Values')
plt.ylabel('Predicted Values')
```

```
plt.title('Predicted vs. Actual Values')
plt.show()
```

Diagnosing Issues:

Beyond evaluating the overall performance, it's crucial to identify and address potential issues with your model:

- **High MSE/RMSE:** A high MSE/RMSE indicates that the model's predictions are generally far from the actual values. This could be due to factors like:

  - **Underfitting:** The model is too simple and hasn't captured the underlying relationships in the data.
  - **Overfitting:** The model has memorized the training data too well and doesn't generalize well to unseen data.
  - **Errors in data collection or preprocessing:** Inaccurate or inconsistent data can lead to poor model performance.
- **Residual Analysis:** Analyzing the residuals (errors between predicted and actual values) can expose issues like:

- **Non-linear relationship:** If the residuals show a pattern (e.g., a curve), it might indicate a non-linear relationship between the features and the target variable, which linear regression can't model effectively.
- **Heteroscedasticity:** If the spread of the residuals isn't constant across the range of predicted values, it suggests heteroscedasticity, which can affect the reliability of statistical tests used to evaluate the model.

The Art of Model Improvement:

Linear regression is a powerful tool, but it's not a magic bullet. By understanding these evaluation metrics and diagnostic techniques, you can iteratively improve your model's performance. This might involve:

- **Data cleaning and preprocessing:** Ensuring your data is accurate and consistent can significantly improve model performance.
- **Feature selection:** Identifying the most relevant features can help reduce noise and improve model generalizability.
- **Model Selection and Tuning:** Exploring different regression techniques (e.g., Ridge or LASSO regression) and tuning hyperparameters can lead to better performance.

Evaluation and diagnosis are ongoing processes. As you gain more experience, you'll develop a keen eye for identifying potential issues and refining your linear regression models for optimal performance.

Hands-on Project: Predicting Real-World Outcomes with Linear Regression

Welcome, intrepid data explorers! Are you ready to put your linear regression skills to the test? This project will guide you through building a model to predict a real-world outcome using Python's scikit-learn library. Get ready to harness the power of linear regression for practical applications!

Choosing Your Prediction Task:

For this project, you have the freedom to explore various real-world scenarios. Here are some ideas to get you started:

- **Stock Price Prediction:** Can you predict future stock prices based on historical data like opening/closing prices, trading volume, and market indicators?

- **Customer Churn Prediction:** By analyzing customer data (purchase history, demographics, etc.), can you identify customers at risk of churning (stopping business with you)?
- **House Price Prediction:** Using features like square footage, location, and number of bedrooms, can you develop a model to predict house prices?

The Dataset Delve:

1. **Find Your Data:** Search online repositories like Kaggle or UCI Machine Learning Repository for datasets that align with your chosen prediction task. Ensure the dataset includes relevant features (independent variables) and the target variable (what you want to predict).

2. **Download and Load the Data:** Download the CSV file containing your chosen dataset. Use pandas read_csv to load the data into a Python dataframe:

Python

```
import pandas as pd
```

```
# Replace 'your_data.csv' with the actual filename
data = pd.read_csv('your_data.csv')
```

3. **Data Exploration and Cleaning:** Get familiar with your data by exploring its structure, identifying missing values, and checking for outliers. Clean and pre-process the data as needed using pandas techniques (e.g., imputing missing values, handling categorical features).

Building the Model:

1. **Feature Selection (Optional):** Depending on the size and complexity of your dataset, you might consider feature selection techniques like correlation analysis or feature importance scores to identify the most relevant features for your prediction task.

2. **Splitting the Data:** Use `train_test_split` from `sklearn.model_selection` to split your data into training and testing sets (e.g., 80% training, 20% testing). The

training set will be used to fit the model, and the testing set will be used to evaluate its performance on unseen data.

Python

```
from           sklearn.model_selection           import
train_test_split

X_train,     X_test,     y_train,     y_test     =
train_test_split(
    data[features],    #  Replace  'features'  with
your list of features
    data[target_variable],           #        Replace
'target_variable' with your target variable name
    test_size=0.2)
```

3. **Model Creation and Training:** Instantiate a `LinearRegression` object from `sklearn.linear_model` and train the model using the `fit` method on the training data:

Python

```
from sklearn.linear_model import LinearRegression

model = LinearRegression()

model.fit(X_train, y_train)
```

Model Evaluation and Refinement:

1. **Making Predictions:** Use the `predict` method to generate predictions for the target variable on the testing data:

Python

```
y_predicted = model.predict(X_test)
```

2. **Evaluation Metrics:** Calculate evaluation metrics like MSE and RMSE to assess the model's performance on unseen data. Libraries like numpy can be used for these calculations (refer to explanations in Chapter 4.3 for code examples).

3. **Model Interpretation:** Analyze the coefficients of the fitted model to understand the direction and strength of the relationships between the features and the target variable. This can provide insights into which features have the most significant impact on the prediction.

4. **Model Improvement (Optional):** Based on the evaluation results and potential diagnostic plots (refer to Chapter 4.3), you can explore techniques like:

    ○ Feature engineering: Creating new features from existing ones to improve model performance.
    ○ Model tuning: Adjusting hyperparameters (e.g., regularization strength) of the linear regression model.
    ○ Trying different regression algorithms: Exploring alternatives like Ridge or LASSO regression if linear relationships aren't well-suited for your data.

This is an iterative process. As you experiment with different techniques and analyze the results, you can refine your model to achieve the best possible prediction performance on unseen data.

Chapter 5: Unveiling the Secrets of Classification

Welcome, intrepid data explorers! In this chapter, we delve into the realm of classification – a branch of machine learning where we predict categorical outcomes. Imagine you're sorting emails into spam and non-spam categories, or classifying customers as high-risk or low-risk for credit card fraud. Classification models are the detectives on the case, meticulously sifting through data to make these crucial distinctions.

5.1 Logistic Regression: The Binary Classification Hero

Linear regression, the champion of predicting continuous values, might leave you wondering: what if we want to predict something categorical? For instance, classifying emails as spam (category 1) or not spam (category 0), or distinguishing between healthy and unhealthy cells in a medical diagnosis. This is where logistic regression steps into the spotlight – the hero for binary classification tasks!

While linear regression spits out continuous numbers, logistic regression builds upon that foundation to tackle categorical outcomes. But how does it achieve this feat? The secret weapon is the **sigmoid function**.

Imagine the sigmoid function as an S-shaped curve that stretches infinitely on both ends but never quite touches the x or y axis. It takes any real number as input and squishes it between 0 (representing a very low probability) and 1 (representing a very high probability).

Here's how logistic regression leverages this powerful function:

1. **Linear Under the Hood:** At its core, logistic regression uses a linear equation, much like linear regression, to model the relationship between the features (independent variables) and the target variable (categorical). This equation assigns a score to each   data   point.

2. **The Sigmoid Shuffle:** The magic happens here! Logistic regression plugs the score from the linear equation into the sigmoid function. This transforms the score into a probability between 0 and 1. In essence, the sigmoid function acts as a translator, converting the raw linear output into a probability that represents the likelihood of belonging to the positive class (category   1).

The Decision Threshold: From Probabilities to Predictions

So far, so good! We have probabilities, but real-world classification demands a definitive answer – spam or not spam? This is where the **decision threshold** comes in. Typically set at 0.5, it acts as a classification boundary.

- **Above the Threshold (Probability > 0.5):** If the predicted probability from the sigmoid function is greater than 0.5, the model classifies the data point as belonging to the positive class (category 1).
- **Below the Threshold (Probability <= 0.5):** Conversely, if the probability is less than or equal to 0.5, the model classifies it as belonging to the negative class (category 0).

Remember, the decision threshold is adjustable! In some cases, the cost of misclassification might be imbalanced. For instance, in credit card fraud detection, a false positive (mistakenly flagging a legitimate transaction) might be less concerning than a false negative (missing a fraudulent transaction). By adjusting the threshold (e.g., raising it to 0.6), you can prioritize minimizing false positives.

Logistic regression is a powerful tool for binary classification, but it's important to remember:

- **It thrives on linearly separable data:** If the data isn't naturally divided by a straight line, logistic regression might struggle.
- **It excels with balanced classes:** When the number of data points in each category is roughly similar, the model performs better.

As you venture further into the world of classification, you'll encounter techniques to handle these limitations and explore algorithms for multi-class classification problems (where there are more than two categories). But for now, logistic regression is a fantastic first step in your classification journey!

5.2 Implementing Logistic Regression with Python (Binary Classification)

Logistic regression is a theoretical powerhouse, but how do we translate that into action? Brace yourself, for we're about to embark on building a logistic regression model using Python's `scikit-learn` library! Get ready to conquer binary classification tasks with code.

The Step-by-Step Guide:

1. **Import the Necessary Libraries:**

Python

```
import pandas as pd

from        sklearn.model_selection        import
train_test_split

from         sklearn.linear_model          import
LogisticRegression
```

- ○ `pandas`: This library is your trusty companion for data manipulation and analysis in Python.
- ○ `train_test_split` from `sklearn.model_selection`: This function helps you split your data into training and testing sets, a crucial step for model evaluation.
- ○ `LogisticRegression` from `sklearn.linear_model`: This is the champion we'll be using to create and train our logistic regression model.

2. **Load and Prepare Your Data:**

- ○ Load your data from a CSV file using pandas `read_csv` (replace 'your_data.csv' with your actual filename):

Python

```
data = pd.read_csv('your_data.csv')
```

- o Identify the features (independent variables) and the target variable (categorical) you want to predict. The target variable should have values representing the two categories (e.g., 0 for negative class, 1 for positive class).

- o Handle missing values (if any) using appropriate techniques like imputation or deletion (depending on your data and analysis goals).

- o Encode categorical features (if any) using techniques like one-hot encoding. One-hot encoding transforms categorical features into numerical representations suitable for logistic regression   models.   Here's   an   example:

Python

```
from sklearn.preprocessing import OneHotEncoder

encoder = OneHotEncoder(sparse=False)

categorical_features = ['feature1', 'feature2']  #
Replace with your categorical features

encoded_data           =           pd.concat([data,
pd.DataFrame(encoder.fit_transform(data[categorica
l_features]))], axis=1)

encoded_data.drop(categorical_features,     axis=1,
inplace=True)     #  Remove  original  categorical
features
```

3. **Splitting the Data into Training and Testing Sets:**
   - Use `train_test_split` to split your encoded data into training and testing sets (e.g., 80% training, 20% testing). The training set will be used to fit the model,

and the testing set will be used to evaluate its
performance on unseen data.

Python

```python
X_train,     X_test,     y_train,     y_test     =
train_test_split(
    encoded_data[features],   # Replace 'features'
with your list of features
    data['target_variable'],          #    Replace
'target_variable' with your target variable name

    test_size=0.2)
```

4. **Creating and Training the Model:** Instantiate a
   `LogisticRegression` object:

Python

```python
model = LogisticRegression()
```

Train the model using the `fit` method. This involves the model learning the coefficients of the linear equation and the sigmoid function parameters that best represent the relationship between the features and the probability of belonging to the positive class.

Python

```python
model.fit(X_train, y_train)
```

Making   Predictions:

Use the `predict_proba` method to generate probability predictions for the target variable on the testing data. This method outputs an array where each element represents the probability of a data point belonging to the positive class (category 1).

Python

```python
y_predicted_proba = model.predict_proba(X_test)
```

Note that y_predicted_proba is a two-dimensional array. The first column contains the probabilities of belonging to the negative class (category 0), and the second column contains the probabilities of belonging to the positive class (category 1). We typically use the values in the second column for further analysis and classification.

Beyond the Predictions:

This code snippet equips you with the power to train a logistic regression model and generate probability predictions. In the next section, we'll delve into evaluation metrics to assess how well your model performs and how to interpret the results to gain insights from your data.

Hands-on Project: Fraud Detection or Customer Segmentation with Logistic Regression

Let's put your newfound logistic regression skills into action! This project tackles a real-world scenario: identifying fraudulent transactions or segmenting customers based on their behavior.

Choosing Your Path:

1. **Fraud Detection:** Imagine you have a dataset containing transaction information (amount, location, time, etc.). Your goal is to build a model that can classify transactions as fraudulent (category 1) or legitimate (category 0) based on historical   data.

2. **Customer Segmentation:** You have data about customer purchases, demographics, and website interactions. By building a logistic regression model, you can classify customers into segments (e.g., high-spending vs. low-spending) to tailor marketing   campaigns   or   personalize   product recommendations.

The Data Delve:

1. **Find Your Data:** Search online repositories like Kaggle or UCI Machine Learning Repository for datasets that align with your chosen task (fraud detection or customer segmentation). Ensure the dataset includes relevant features and a categorical target variable indicating the category (e.g., fraudulent/legitimate for fraud detection or customer segment labels for segmentation).

2. **Download and Load the Data:** Download the CSV file containing your chosen dataset. Use pandas `read_csv` to load the data into a Python dataframe:

Python

```python
import pandas as pd

# Replace 'your_data.csv' with the actual filename
data = pd.read_csv('your_data.csv')
```

3. **Data Exploration and Cleaning:** Get familiar with your data by exploring its structure, identifying missing values, and checking for outliers. Clean and pre-process the data as needed using pandas techniques (e.g., imputing missing values, handling categorical features).

Building the Model:

1. **Feature Selection (Optional):** Depending on the size and complexity of your dataset, you might consider feature selection techniques like correlation analysis or feature importance scores to identify the most relevant features for your prediction task.

2. **Splitting the Data:** Use `train_test_split` from `sklearn.model_selection` to split your data into training and testing sets (e.g., 80% training, 20% testing). The training set will be used to fit the model, and the testing set will be used to evaluate its performance on unseen data.

Python

```python
from        sklearn.model_selection         import
train_test_split

X_train,    X_test,     y_train,    y_test    =
train_test_split(
    data[features],   # Replace 'features' with
your list of features
    data[target_variable],          # Replace
'target_variable' with your target variable name
    test_size=0.2)
```

3. **Model Creation and Training:** Instantiate a
   `LogisticRegression` object from `sklearn.linear_model` and
   train the model using the `fit` method on the training data:

Python

```python
from sklearn.linear_model import
LogisticRegression

model = LogisticRegression()
```

```
model.fit(X_train, y_train)
```

Model Evaluation and Interpretation:

1. **Making Predictions:** Use the `predict_proba` method to generate probability predictions for the target variable on the testing data:

Python

```
y_predicted_proba = model.predict_proba(X_test)[:,
1]  # Select probabilities for positive class
```

We use `[:, 1]` to select the probabilities for the positive class (category 1) from the two-dimensional array returned by `predict_proba`.

2. **Evaluation Metrics:** Calculate evaluation metrics like accuracy, precision, and recall to assess the model's

performance on unseen data. Libraries like `scikit-learn` provide functions for these calculations (refer to Chapter 5.3 for explanations and code examples).

3. **Decision Threshold:** Set a decision threshold (typically 0.5) to classify data points based on the predicted probabilities. For instance, a data point with a predicted probability of 0.65 (above the threshold) might be classified as fraudulent in a fraud detection scenario.

4. **Model Interpretation (Optional):** Analyze the coefficients of the fitted model to understand the impact of different features on the probability of belonging to the positive class. This can provide insights into which features are most indicative of fraudulent transactions or specific customer segments.

Beyond the Code:

• **Fine-tuning the Model:** Based on the evaluation results, you can explore techniques like adjusting hyperparameters (regularization strength) or trying different classification algorithms to improve model performance.

Visualization Power:

- **ROC Curves:** Go beyond accuracy and explore Receiver Operating Characteristic (ROC) curves. These curves visualize the trade-off between true positive rate (correctly identifying positive cases) and false positive rate (incorrectly identifying negative cases). A higher ROC AUC (Area Under the Curve) signifies better model performance at distinguishing between categories.

    - Libraries like `scikit-learn` provide functions for generating ROC curves. Search online for tutorials and interpretations of ROC curves in classification tasks.

- **Confusion Matrix:** Create a confusion matrix to visualize the model's performance in a clear table format. Rows represent actual categories, and columns represent predicted categories. This helps identify potential areas for improvement (e.g., high number of false negatives in fraud detection).

Chapter 6: Taming the Complexity: Beyond Linear Models

While linear regression and logistic regression have proven their worth, the world of data isn't always so linear. Imagine you're trying to predict house prices – there might be complex relationships between factors like location, size, and amenities that a straight line can't quite capture. This is where we venture beyond linear models and explore more flexible approaches, like decision trees.

6.1 Limitations of Linear Models and the Need for More Flexible Approaches

Linear regression and logistic regression have been our trusty companions in uncovering patterns and making predictions. But, as data scientists, we yearn to explore more complex relationships lurking within our data. Just like a map with only straight lines wouldn't accurately represent a winding mountain road, linear models sometimes struggle to capture the intricacies of the real world.

Here's a closer look at the limitations of linear models that motivate us to seek more flexible approaches:

1. **Limited Explanatory Power:** Linear models excel at capturing linear relationships between features and the target variable. Imagine predicting house prices based on square footage. A linear model can handle this with ease. However, what if the relationship becomes more complex? For instance, location might play a significant role, and houses in a specific neighborhood might command higher prices even with lower square footage. Linear models struggle to capture these non-linear patterns effectively.

   - Consider a scenario where you're trying to predict customer churn (cancelling a subscription). A linear model might assume a steady increase in churn probability with decreasing customer satisfaction. In reality, the relationship might be more nuanced, with churn probability spiking dramatically only when satisfaction falls below a certain threshold.

2. **Feature Interactions:** Linear models treat features as independent entities. This means they assume there's no interaction or combined effect between features. Going back to the house price example, the combined effect of location and square footage might be more significant than their individual contributions. A linear model wouldn't be able to

capture   this   interaction.

3. **Sensitivity to Outliers:** Outliers – data points that fall far from the majority – can significantly impact the coefficients of a linear model. This can skew the model's predictions and lead to   inaccurate   results.

The Quest for Flexibility: These limitations highlight the need for models that can adapt to the complexities of real-world data. We need models that can capture non-linear relationships, account for feature interactions, and be less susceptible to outliers. This is where our journey towards more flexible approaches, like decision trees, begins!

6.2 Introduction to Decision Trees:

We've identified the limitations of linear models, and the call for a more flexible approach is loud and clear. Enter decision trees, powerful tools that bring a breath of fresh air to the world of machine learning!

Imagine a flowchart, but instead of following a pre-defined path, you navigate based on a series of questions about the features in your data. These questions lead you to different branches, ultimately reaching a final decision. That's the essence of a decision tree!

Here's a breakdown of the key components that make decision trees tick:

- **Root Node:** This is the starting point of the tree, representing the entire dataset. Think of it as the grand entrance hall in our flowchart   analogy.

- **Internal Nodes:** These nodes act as decision points, asking questions about specific features in your data. The answer to each question determines how the data is split into further branches. Imagine these as decision points in the flowchart, with arrows leading to different sections based on your answer (Yes/No   or   specific   value   ranges).

- **Leaf Nodes:** These represent the final destinations in the tree. They contain instances from the data that share similar characteristics based on the decisions made along the way. In our flowchart analogy, these are the end points where you reach a specific conclusion. In classification trees, leaf nodes represent categories (e.g., fraudulent/legitimate transaction). In regression trees, they represent ranges of values for the target variable (e.g., house price range).

- **The Interpretability Advantage:** One of the biggest advantages of decision trees is their interpretability. Unlike some complex models that treat data as a black box, decision trees offer transparency. By following the splits and questions throughout the tree, you can understand the decision-making process and how different features contribute to the final predictions. This allows you to gain valuable insights into the relationships between features and the target variable.

Making a Decision:

So, how exactly do decision trees make decisions and split the data? They use a specific criterion to evaluate which feature and which split point will result in the most homogeneous subgroups in terms of the target variable:

- **Classification:** The Gini impurity measure is commonly used. It essentially calculates how well-mixed the classes are within a particular node. The decision tree strives to make splits that result in the purest possible groups at the leaf nodes (i.e., containing mostly data points from one class).

- **Regression:** Mean squared error (MSE) or variance reduction are often used. These measures evaluate how much the split reduces the overall squared error (difference between predicted and actual values) or variance in the target variable within each subgroup.

By iteratively splitting the data based on these criteria, decision trees build a hierarchical structure that captures complex relationships within the data. This makes them a powerful tool for tackling tasks where linear models might fall short.

6.3 Implementing Decision Trees using Python (Classification & Regression)

Linear models may have served us well so far, but their limitations push us to explore more versatile tools. Decision trees, with their ability to capture intricate data patterns, are ready to take center stage! Let's leverage Python's `scikit-learn` library to build decision trees for both classification and regression tasks.

The Step-by-Step Guide:

1. **Import the Necessary Libraries:**

Python

```python
import pandas as pd

from sklearn.model_selection import train_test_split

from sklearn.tree import DecisionTreeClassifier  # for classification

from sklearn.tree import DecisionTreeRegressor  # for regression
```

We'll import `pandas` for data manipulation and `train_test_split` from `sklearn.model_selection` to split our data into training and testing sets.

Note that `scikit-learn` provides separate decision tree implementations for classification (`DecisionTreeClassifier`) and regression (`DecisionTreeRegressor`).

2. Load and Prepare Your Data:

Follow the same steps from previous chapters to load your data from a CSV file using pandas `read_csv` and perform any necessary cleaning and pre-processing. Ensure your data is in a suitable format for the chosen task (classification or regression).

3. Splitting the Data:

Use `train_test_split` to split your prepared data into training and testing sets. This helps us evaluate the model's performance on unseen data.

4. Creating and Training the Model:

Classification:

Python

```python
model = DecisionTreeClassifier()
model.fit(X_train, y_train)
```

Here, we instantiate a `DecisionTreeClassifier` object and train it using the `fit` method. The model will learn the decision rules based on the features (X_train) and the target variable categories (y_train).

Regression:

Python

```python
model = DecisionTreeRegressor()
model.fit(X_train, y_train)
```

Similarly, for regression tasks, we create a `DecisionTreeRegressor` object and train it using the `fit` method on the training data (X_train represents features, and y_train represents the continuous target variable values).

5. **Making Predictions:**

Once the model is trained, you can use the `predict` method to generate predictions on the testing data:

Python

```
y_predicted = model.predict(X_test)
```

This provides the predicted categories (classification) or predicted values (regression) for the data points in X_test.

Decision trees offer a powerful approach to data analysis, but there's more to explore! Here are some additional points to consider:

- **Hyperparameter Tuning:** Decision trees have hyperparameters, like the maximum depth of the tree, that control its complexity. Tuning these hyperparameters can significantly impact the model's performance. scikit-learn provides tools for grid search and randomized search to find optimal hyperparameter settings.

- **Ensemble Methods:** While a single decision tree can be powerful, combining multiple decision trees using techniques like Random Forest can often improve performance and stability. Random Forests create multiple decision trees with some variations (e.g., randomly selecting features at each split) and average their predictions, leading to a more robust model.

Hands-on Project: Decision Trees vs. Linear Regression

This project throws down the gauntlet, pitting linear regression and decision trees against each other! We'll compare their performance on a dataset of your choice, helping you understand their strengths and weaknesses in different scenarios.

Step 1: Choosing Your Dataset

1. **Classification or Regression?** The first step is to select a dataset that aligns with your preferred task:

   - **Classification:** Examples include predicting customer churn (churn vs. not churn), classifying spam emails (spam vs. not spam), or loan approval (approved vs. rejected).
   - **Regression:** If you're interested in predicting continuous values, explore house price prediction, stock price prediction, or customer lifetime value prediction datasets.

2. Remember, the chosen dataset should have relevant features and a target variable that matches your task (categorical for classification, continuous for regression). Websites like Kaggle (https://www.kaggle.com/) and UCI Machine Learning

Repository (https://archive.ics.uci.edu/) are great resources for finding datasets.

3. **Download and Explore:** Once you've identified your champion dataset, download the CSV file. Use a text editor to get a basic understanding of the features and target variable.

Step 2: Data Preparation

1. **Load the Data:** Use pandas (`import pandas as pd`) to load the CSV data into a DataFrame.

Python

```
data = pd.read_csv("your_dataset.csv")
```

2. **Handle Missing Values:** Check for missing values using `data.isnull().sum()`. Common techniques for handling missing values include filling with mean/median values or dropping rows/columns with too many missing

entries (depending on the context).

3. **Process Categorical Features (Classification):** If you're working on a classification task and have categorical features, you'll need to encode them for the model to understand. One-hot encoding or label encoding are common techniques. Libraries like `scikit-learn` provide functions for these tasks.

4. **Scale Numerical Features (if necessary):** Depending on the models you choose, scaling numerical features to a common range might be necessary (e.g., using StandardScaler from `scikit-learn`). This ensures all features contribute equally to the model's learning process.

Step 3: Splitting the Data

1. **Import Libraries:** Import `train_test_split` from `sklearn.model_selection` to split your data into training and testing sets.

Python

```
from        sklearn.model_selection        import
train_test_split
```

2. **Split:** Use `train_test_split` to create training and testing sets. A typical split is 80% for training and 20% for testing.

Python

```
X_train,    X_test,    y_train,    y_test    =
train_test_split(data.drop("target_variable",
axis=1),  # Features (all columns except target)

data["target_variable"],  # Target variable

test_size=0.2,  # 20% for testing

random_state=42)  # For reproducibility
```

Step 4: Building and Evaluating Models

Linear Regression (if applicable):

1. **Create the Model:** Import `LinearRegression` from `sklearn.linear_model` and create an instance.

Python

```python
from sklearn.linear_model import LinearRegression
model_linear = LinearRegression()
```

2. **Train the Model:** Train the model on the training data using the `fit` method.

Python

```python
model_linear.fit(X_train, y_train)
```

3. **Make Predictions:** Use the `predict` method to generate predictions on the testing data.

Python

```python
y_predicted_linear = model_linear.predict(X_test)
```

4. **Evaluation:** Evaluate the model's performance using metrics like mean squared error (MSE) or root mean squared error (RMSE) for regression tasks. Libraries like `sklearn.metrics` provide functions for these calculations.

Decision Tree (Classification or Regression):

1. **Create the Model:** Import `DecisionTreeClassifier` (for classification) or `DecisionTreeRegressor` (for regression) from `sklearn.tree` and create an instance.

Python

```
from sklearn.tree import DecisionTreeClassifier   #
or DecisionTreeRegressor for regression
model_tree = DecisionTreeClassifier
```

2. **Train the Model:** Train the model on the training data using the `fit` method.

Python

```
model_tree.fit(X_train, y_train)
```

2. **Make Predictions:** Use the `predict` method to generate predictions on the testing data.

Python

```
y_predicted_tree = model_tree.predict(X_test)
```

3. **Evaluation:** Evaluate the model's performance using relevant metrics:

Classification: Use `classification_report` and `accuracy_score` from `sklearn.metrics` to get metrics like accuracy, precision, recall, and F1-score. These provide insights into how well the model identifies true positives, avoids false positives/negatives, and balances these factors.

Python

```
from sklearn.metrics import classification_report,
accuracy_score
print(classification_report(y_test, y_predicted_tree))

print("Accuracy:", accuracy_score(y_test, y_predicted_tree))
```

Regression: Use the same metrics (MSE/RMSE) as you did for linear regression (if applicable).

Step 5: Comparison and Analysis

1. **Analyze Results:** Compare the performance of the linear regression and decision tree models based on the chosen metrics. Did one model outperform the other?

2. **Consider Complexity:** If the data has complex, non-linear relationships, the decision tree might have been better equipped to capture them compared to linear regression.

3. **Feature Interactions:** Decision trees can handle interactions between features, which might be advantageous if such interactions exist in the data.

Step 6: Bonus Exploration

1. **Decision Tree Visualization (Classification):** For classification tasks, explore visualizing the decision tree using libraries like `graphviz` or `matplotlib`. This can provide insights into the decision rules learned by the model.

2. **Hyperparameter Tuning:** Both models have hyperparameters you can adjust to potentially improve performance. Experiment with hyperparameter tuning for decision trees (e.g., maximum depth) and linear regression

(e.g., regularization parameters) using techniques like grid search or randomized search from `scikit-learn`.

There's no single "best" model for every situation. This project equips you to compare decision trees and linear regression and understand their strengths and weaknesses on different datasets. As you explore more complex datasets and tasks, you'll have a better understanding of which model to choose for optimal performance.

Part 3: Advanced Techniques for Real-World Applications

Chapter 7: Ensemble Learning: Strength in Numbers

We've conquered linear regression and decision trees, but what if there was a way to harness the power of multiple models for even better results? Enter ensemble learning, a powerful approach that combines the predictions of multiple models to create a stronger, more robust learner. Imagine a team of experts collaborating to solve a problem – that's the essence of ensemble methods.

This chapter delves into two popular ensemble techniques: Random Forests and Gradient Boosting. We'll explore their inner workings, understand their advantages, and equip you with Python code to implement them for enhanced prediction tasks.

7.1 The Power of Many: Why Ensemble Learning?

We've wielded the power of linear regression and decision trees, but what if we could combine their strengths to create an even more powerful learner? Ensemble learning offers a compelling answer. Imagine a team of experts collaborating to solve a complex problem – that's the core idea behind ensemble methods. They combine the predictions from multiple models to create a stronger, more robust learner.

This chapter dives into the world of ensemble learning, exploring two popular techniques: Random Forests and Gradient Boosting. We'll unveil their inner workings, understand their advantages, and equip you with Python code to leverage them for enhanced prediction tasks.

But before we delve deeper, why exactly should we consider ensemble methods? Here are some key benefits that might surprise you:

- **Superior Accuracy:** By harnessing the collective wisdom of multiple models, ensembles can often achieve significantly higher accuracy compared to any single model. Think of it as leveraging a broader range of perspectives to arrive at a more comprehensive solution.

- **Reduced Variance:** Ensemble methods have a trick up their sleeve to combat variance, a measure of how sensitive a model's predictions are to small changes in the data. By averaging the predictions from individual models (which might have some randomness in their decisions), ensembles can reduce the overall influence of noise in the data and lead to more stable predictions. Imagine multiple advisors providing slightly different recommendations – the ensemble takes an average, leading to a more consistent outcome.

- **Tackling Complex Problems:** The world is full of intricate problems with non-linear relationships between features and the target variable. While a single decision tree might struggle with such complexities, ensemble methods can rise to the challenge. By combining diverse models, they can capture these intricate relationships and deliver superior results.

The Secret Ingredient: Diversity

A critical aspect of ensemble learning lies in ensuring diversity among the base models (the individual models that make up the ensemble). Just like a team thrives on a variety of perspectives, an ensemble benefits from having models that approach the problem from different angles. Diverse models are less likely to make the same mistakes, leading to a more robust ensemble that can generalize better to unseen data. The next sections will explore how Random Forests and Gradient Boosting achieve this diversity.

7.2 Random Forests: Wisdom of the Crowd

Have you ever gotten lost in a forest? While that might not be ideal in real life, the concept of a random forest is a powerful tool in machine learning. Here, a random forest isn't a navigational nightmare, but rather an ensemble method that builds upon the wisdom of a crowd – a crowd of decision trees!

Random Forests create multiple decision trees, each with a unique twist: they are trained on a random subset of features and data points. This injects diversity into the ensemble, preventing the trees from becoming too similar and potentially falling prey to overfitting.

Let's delve into the inner workings of a random forest:

1. **Bootstrapping the Data:** Random Forests leverage a technique called bootstrapping to create multiple training sets for the decision trees. Think of it like randomly grabbing handfuls of data points (with replacement) from a bag – some data points might appear multiple times in a single handful, while others might be left out entirely. This creates new training sets, each with the same size as the original dataset but with variations that lead to diverse learning experiences for the

decision   trees.

2. **Random Feature Selection:** While a traditional decision tree considers all features at each split point, Random Forests introduce another layer of randomness. For each decision tree, a random subset of features is chosen as candidates for splitting the data at each node. This injects further diversity into the trees, as they learn to make decisions based on different combinations   of   features.

3. **Majority Vote (Classification) or Averaging (Regression):** Once all the trees in the forest are trained, it's prediction time! For classification tasks, the ensemble predicts the class that receives the most votes from the individual trees. Imagine a group of experts voting on a decision – the random forest chooses the class with the most votes from its "forest" of experts (the decision trees). For regression tasks, the ensemble prediction is the average of the predictions from all the trees in the forest. Here, the wisdom of the crowd prevails, with the final prediction reflecting the average output of all the trees.

The Power of Diversity: By combining these elements – bootstrapping, random feature selection, and voting/averaging – Random Forests create a powerful ensemble. The diversity among the trees helps reduce variance, avoids overfitting, and often leads to more accurate and generalizable predictions compared to a single decision tree.

Ready to Code a Random Forest?

Let's leverage Python's `scikit-learn` library to see how we can create a random forest in action:

Python

```python
from           sklearn.ensemble              import
RandomForestClassifier  # for classification

from sklearn.ensemble import RandomForestRegressor
# for regression



# ... (data preparation and train-test split)



# Create a random forest with 100 decision trees

model = RandomForestClassifier(n_estimators=100)
```

```
# Train the model on the training data
model.fit(X_train, y_train)


# Use the model to make predictions on the testing
data
y_predicted = model.predict(X_test)
```

This code snippet creates a random forest with 100 decision trees and trains it on your prepared data. The `predict` method allows you to use the trained model to generate predictions on new, unseen data.

By harnessing the wisdom of the crowd – the diverse collection of decision trees – random forests offer a powerful approach to enhance the accuracy and robustness of your machine learning models.

7.3 Gradient Boosting: Sequential Learners

Random Forests create a powerful ensemble by leveraging a "democratic" approach, where multiple decision trees are trained independently. But what if we could create an ensemble where the models learn from each other in a sequential way? This is the core idea behind Gradient Boosting, another prominent ensemble learning technique.

Think of Gradient Boosting as a team of students working on a problem together. The first student takes a stab at solving it, and then the next student builds upon the first one's work, trying to correct any errors. This collaborative learning process continues until the team arrives at a much better solution.

Here's a breakdown of how Gradient Boosting achieves this:

1. **Stage-wise Approach:** Unlike Random Forests, Gradient Boosting builds models in a step-by-step manner. It starts with a simple model (often a decision tree) and then iteratively adds new models to the ensemble. Each new model is specifically designed to address the shortcomings of the previous models.

2. **Learning from Errors:** The key to Gradient Boosting's effectiveness lies in how it trains each new model. Instead of using the original data for training, each new model focuses on the **errors** made by the previous models. The goal is to learn

from these errors and improve the overall prediction accuracy.

3. **Boosting the Signal:** This sequential approach, where each model learns from the errors of its predecessors, helps "boost" the overall signal and reduce the impact of noise in the data. Imagine a team of experts iteratively refining their understanding of a problem – Gradient Boosting works in a similar way, gradually improving the ensemble's performance with each new model.

Gradient Boosting Techniques:

There are several popular Gradient Boosting implementations, with slight variations in their approach. Two prominent ones include:

- **Gradient Boosting Machines (GBMs):** This technique uses decision trees as the base learners and employs a specific algorithm to determine how much weight to give to each new model in the ensemble.

- **XGBoost:** An extension of GBMs, XGBoost offers additional features like regularization and support for various objective functions, making it a powerful tool for a wider range of machine				learning				tasks.

We'll explore implementing Gradient Boosting using scikit-learn's GradientBoostingClassifier (for classification) or GradientBoostingRegressor (for regression) in the next section. However, it's important to note that these implementations might not offer the full feature set of advanced techniques like XGBoost.

Ready to Try Gradient Boosting?

The code structure for implementing Gradient Boosting with scikit-learn is similar to Random Forests, but with some key differences in the model selection process. We'll cover the specifics in the next section.

7.4 Implementing Ensemble Methods with Python

We've explored the inner workings of Random Forests and Gradient Boosting. Now, let's leverage Python's `scikit-learn` library to put these ensemble methods into action!

Random Forests:

As we saw earlier, Random Forests are built using the RandomForestClassifier (for classification) or RandomForestRegressor (for regression) classes from scikit-learn. Here's a breakdown of the code and some key points to remember:

Python

```python
from sklearn.ensemble import RandomForestClassifier  # for classification

from sklearn.ensemble import RandomForestRegressor # for regression


# ... (your data preparation and train-test split code)


# Create a random forest with 100 decision trees

model = RandomForestClassifier(n_estimators=100)


# Train the model on the training data

model.fit(X_train, y_train)
```

```
# Use the model to make predictions on the testing
data

y_predicted = model.predict(X_test)
```

- n_estimators: This parameter specifies the number of decision trees to be included in the forest. Experimenting with different values can help optimize performance for your specific dataset.
- **Randomness is Key:** Remember, randomness is a core aspect of Random Forests. The fit method internally handles bootstrapping data samples and random feature selection at each split point.

Gradient Boosting:

scikit-learn provides GradientBoostingClassifier and GradientBoostingRegressor for classification and regression tasks, respectively. Here's an example for classification:

Python

```python
from sklearn.ensemble import
GradientBoostingClassifier

# ... (your data preparation and train-test split
code)

# Create a Gradient Boosting model with 100 trees
model =
GradientBoostingClassifier(n_estimators=100)

# Train the model on the training data
model.fit(X_train, y_train)

# Use the model to make predictions on the testing
data
y_predicted = model.predict(X_test)
```

Key Differences from Random Forests:

- **No Random Subsets:** Unlike Random Forests, Gradient Boosting doesn't use bootstrapping or random feature selection during training. It focuses on sequentially adding models to improve upon the ensemble's performance.

- `learning_rate` **Hyperparameter:** Gradient Boosting algorithms often have a `learning_rate` hyperparameter. This controls how much weight each new model contributes to the ensemble. Experimenting with different values can help fine-tune the model's performance.

Beyond scikit-learn:

While scikit-learn provides basic implementations of Gradient Boosting, advanced techniques like XGBoost offer additional functionalities and often outperform scikit-learn's versions. Exploring these advanced libraries can be beneficial for complex tasks.

Remember:

These code examples provide a starting point. As you explore different datasets and tasks, experiment with hyperparameter tuning (e.g., `n_estimators` for Random Forests, `learning_rate` for Gradient Boosting) to optimize the performance of your ensemble models.

By harnessing the power of ensemble methods like Random Forests and Gradient Boosting, you can unlock new levels of accuracy and robustness in your machine learning projects. So, go forth and explore the wisdom of the crowd!

Hands-on Project: Decision Tree vs. Random Forest

This project puts decision trees and Random Forests head-to-head to assess their predictive prowess. We'll use a real-world dataset and Python's `scikit-learn` library to compare their performance on a classification task.

Dataset:

For this project, we'll use the Iris flower classification dataset, a popular benchmark in machine learning. This dataset contains features of iris flowers (Sepal Length, Sepal Width, Petal Length, Petal Width) belonging to three distinct species: Iris Setosa, Iris Versicolor, and Iris Virginica. Our goal is to build models that can accurately predict the flower species based on these features.

Steps:

1. **Import   Libraries   and   Load   Data:**

Python

```
from sklearn.datasets import load_iris
```

```python
from sklearn.model_selection import
train_test_split
from sklearn.tree import DecisionTreeClassifier
from sklearn.ensemble import
RandomForestClassifier
from sklearn.metrics import accuracy_score

# Load the Iris dataset
iris = load_iris()

# Separate features (X) and target variable (y)
X = iris.data
y = iris.target
```

We import necessary libraries: `load_iris` to fetch the dataset, `train_test_split` for splitting data, `DecisionTreeClassifier` and `RandomForestClassifier` for building models, and `accuracy_score` to evaluate performance.

2. Split Data into Training and Testing Sets:

Python

```python
# Split data into training (80%) and testing (20%)
sets
```

```
X_train, X_test, y_train, y_test =
train_test_split(X, y, test_size=0.2,
random_state=42)
```

This splits the data into training and testing sets. The training set (80%) will be used to train the models, while the testing set (20%) will be used to evaluate their performance on unseen data. Splitting the data ensures a more objective evaluation. We set `random_state=42` for reproducibility (ensuring the same split each time you run the code).

3. **Build and Train a Decision Tree Model:**

Python

```
# Create a decision tree classifier
model_tree = DecisionTreeClassifier()

# Train the model on the training data
model_tree.fit(X_train, y_train)
```

Here, we create a `DecisionTreeClassifier` instance and train it on the training data using the `fit` method.

4. Make Predictions with the Decision Tree:

Python

```python
# Generate predictions on the testing data
y_predicted_tree = model_tree.predict(X_test)
```

We use the trained decision tree model (`model_tree`) to predict the flower species for the testing data points using the `predict` method.

5. Evaluate Decision Tree Performance:

Python

```python
# Calculate the accuracy score
accuracy_tree = accuracy_score(y_test,
y_predicted_tree)
```

```
print("Decision Tree Accuracy:", accuracy_tree)
```

Now, we evaluate the decision tree's performance using the `accuracy_score` function. This function compares the predicted labels (`y_predicted_tree`) with the actual labels (`y_test`) and calculates the percentage of correctly classified instances. The printed result shows the decision tree's accuracy on the unseen testing data.

6. **Build and Train a Random Forest Model:**

Python

```
# Create a random forest classifier with 100 trees
model_forest =
RandomForestClassifier(n_estimators=100)

# Train the model on the training data
model_forest.fit(X_train, y_train)
```

Similar to the decision tree, we create a `RandomForestClassifier` instance, but this time specifying `n_estimators=100` to create a forest with 100 decision trees. We then train the model on the training data.

7. Make Predictions with the Random Forest:

Python

```python
# Generate predictions on the testing data
y_predicted_forest = model_forest.predict(X_test)
```

We use the trained random forest model (`model_forest`) to generate predictions for the testing data using the `predict` method.

8. Evaluate Random Forest Performance:

Python

```python
# Calculate the accuracy score
accuracy_forest    =    accuracy_score(y_test,
y_predicted_forest)

print("Random Forest Accuracy:",
```

Chapter 8: Unveiling the Hidden Patterns: Unsupervised Learning

So far, we've delved into the world of supervised learning, where we have labeled data and train models to make predictions. But what if we have unlabeled data – a treasure trove of information without predefined categories? This is where unsupervised learning steps in, acting like a detective seeking hidden patterns and structures within the data.

Imagine a vast ocean of unlabeled data points. Unsupervised learning techniques are like deep-sea explorers, uncovering natural groupings, relationships, and underlying patterns that might not be readily apparent. This chapter dives into a powerful unsupervised technique: K-Means Clustering.

8.1 Beyond Labels: The Power of Unsupervised Learning

In our machine learning journey so far, we've wielded the power of supervised learning to make predictions. We trained models using labeled data, where each data point has a corresponding category or value we want to predict. But what if we have a treasure trove of data – emails, customer profiles, website clickstreams – that lacks these predefined labels? This is where unsupervised learning steps in, acting like an explorer venturing into uncharted territory.

Unsupervised learning deals with unlabeled data, where the goal is to uncover hidden patterns, structures, and relationships within the data itself. It's like sifting through a collection of seashells – you might not know their exact names or purposes yet, but unsupervised learning can help you identify distinct groups based on size, color, or texture.

Here are some key benefits of unsupervised learning that make it a valuable tool in your data science arsenal:

- **Data Exploration and Discovery:** Unsupervised learning techniques excel at helping you explore and understand your data. They can identify hidden patterns, relationships between features, and natural groupings that you might not have noticed before. Imagine finding clusters of similar seashells based on their characteristics, even if you don't know the specific types of shells yet. This initial exploration can be crucial for formulating hypotheses and guiding further analysis.

- **Dimensionality Reduction:** When dealing with high-dimensional data (data with many features), unsupervised learning techniques can help simplify things. By identifying underlying structures and patterns, they can potentially reduce the number of features needed for analysis. Think of it as summarizing a complex seashell collection by its key characteristics (color, spiral pattern), making it easier to grasp the overall picture. This dimensionality reduction can improve the efficiency and accuracy of other machine learning algorithms.

- **Customer Segmentation:** Unsupervised learning is a game-changer for customer segmentation. By grouping customers with similar characteristics or behavior patterns into distinct clusters, it allows you to tailor marketing campaigns, product recommendations, and overall customer experiences. Imagine segmenting your customers based on their website browsing habits – unsupervised learning can help identify clusters of customers who frequently view travel pages or those who focus on product reviews. This allows you to target your messaging and offerings more effectively.

Unsupervised learning opens doors to a world of possibilities for understanding your data and uncovering valuable insights. The next sections will delve into a powerful technique – K-Means Clustering – that plays a starring role in unsupervised learning.

8.2 K-Means Clustering: Unveiling Natural Groups

Have you ever organized your sock drawer by color? Congratulations, you've intuitively performed a form of clustering! K-Means Clustering, a fundamental unsupervised learning technique, works in a similar way, but for high-dimensional data. It excels at grouping data points into a predefined number of clusters (think color categories for your socks).

Here's a breakdown of how K-Means Clustering works:

1. **Choosing the Number of Clusters (K):** This is a critical step. K-Means needs to know upfront how many clusters (groups) to create in your data. In the sock drawer analogy, this would be deciding on the number of color categories (3 for red, blue, and black, or maybe 10 for more specific shades). Choosing the optimal K often involves experimentation and evaluation using metrics we'll explore later.

2. **Initial Centroids:** K-Means starts by randomly selecting K data points as initial cluster centers, also known as centroids. Imagine placing K empty bins in your drawer – these centroids represent the "cores" of where your socks (data points) will eventually   reside.

3. **Assigning Data Points:** Each data point is assigned to the cluster with the nearest centroid. Think of grabbing a sock and placing it in the bin with the closest color match. K-Means calculates the distance between each data point and all the centroids, assigning the data point to the cluster with the shortest   distance.

4. **Recalculating Centroids:** Once all data points are assigned to a cluster, K-Means takes a step back and reevaluates the centroids. The centroid for each cluster is recalculated as the average of all the data points within that cluster. Imagine taking the average color of all the socks in a bin – this becomes the   new   centroid   for   that   color   category.

5. **Repeating Until Convergence:** Steps 3 and 4 (assigning data points and recalculating centroids) are like a dance that continues until the music stops (or in K-Means terms, until

convergence). Convergence happens when the centroids no longer change significantly, indicating that the clusters have stabilized. This iterative process ensures the clusters refine themselves until they achieve a (hopefully) optimal grouping of the data points.

By iteratively refining the centroids and reassigning data points, K-Means helps us uncover natural groupings within the data. However, it's important to remember that K-Means assumes that the clusters are spherical – like well-defined color clusters in our sock drawer analogy. If your data has more complex cluster shapes, other unsupervised learning techniques might be a better fit.

The Art (and Science) of Choosing K

Choosing the optimal number of clusters (K) is an art and a science. Here are some tips:

- **Experimentation:** Try different K values and evaluate the results using metrics like the Silhouette Coefficient (refer to online resources for details). This will help you identify the K that yields the most distinct and meaningful clusters.

- **Elbow Method:** This technique involves plotting the sum of squared distances between data points and their assigned centroids for different K values. The "elbow" in the plot often indicates a good choice for K, as it suggests a point where adding more clusters doesn't significantly improve the clustering.

K-Means in Action: Python Code Example

Let's leverage Python's `scikit-learn` library to see K-Means Clustering in action:

Python

```python
from sklearn.cluster import KMeans

import matplotlib.pyplot as plt

# ... (your data preparation code)

# Define the number of clusters (experiment with
different values)

n_clusters = 3

# Create a KMeans model with the specified number
of clusters

kmeans = KMeans(n_clusters=n_clusters)
```

```
# Train the model on the data (fitting the data to
the clusters)

kmeans.fit(X)

# Get cluster labels for each data point

cluster_labels = kmeans.labels_

#  ...  (data  visualization  code  using  cluster
labels)
```

This code snippet provides a basic structure for K-Means with `scikit-learn`:

1. Import necessary libraries (`KMeans` for clustering and `matplotlib` for visualization, though visualization isn't covered in this specific code).
2. Define the number of clusters (`n_clusters`).
3. Create a `KMeans` model with the chosen `n_clusters`.
4. Train the model on your data using the `fit` method.
5. Access the cluster labels for each data point using `kmeans.labels_`. This tells you which cluster each data point belongs to.

8.3 Implementing K-Means Clustering with Python

K-Means Clustering offers a powerful tool for uncovering hidden segments within your data. Let's leverage Python's `scikit-learn` library to see how we can implement K-Means for customer segmentation:

Scenario: Imagine you run an e-commerce store and have customer data that includes purchase history, demographics, and website browsing behavior. You'd like to group customers with similar characteristics into distinct segments to personalize marketing campaigns and product recommendations.

Data Preparation:

1. **Import Libraries:**

Python

```python
import pandas as pd
from sklearn.cluster import KMeans
```

We'll use `pandas` for data manipulation and `KMeans` for clustering.

2. **Load Customer Data:**

Python

```
# Load your customer data into a pandas DataFrame
(replace 'path/to/data.csv' with your actual file
path)
data = pd.read_csv('path/to/data.csv')
```

Replace `'path/to/data.csv'` with the actual path to your customer   data   file.

3. **Select Relevant Features:**

Python

```
# Choose features relevant to customer
segmentation (e.g., purchase history,
demographics)
X = data[['feature1', 'feature2', ...]]
```

Replace 'feature1', 'feature2', etc. with the actual column names in your data that best represent customer characteristics. These features will be used for clustering.

K-Means Clustering:

1. **Define the Number of Clusters (K):**

Python

```
# Experiment with different values of K (e.g., 3,
4, 5) to identify optimal segmentation
n_clusters = 3
```

This defines the number of customer segments you want to create. Experiment with different values of n_clusters to see which one yields the most meaningful segmentation for your data.

2. Create and Train the K-Means Model:

Python

```
# Create a KMeans model with the specified number
of clusters
kmeans = KMeans(n_clusters=n_clusters)

# Train the model on the customer data (X)
kmeans.fit(X)
```

Here, we create a KMeans object specifying the number of clusters (n_clusters). Then, we use the fit method to train the model on the prepared   customer   data   (X).

3. Assign Cluster Labels to Customers:

Python

```
# Get the cluster labels for each customer
cluster_labels = kmeans.labels_

# Add a new column to the DataFrame to store the cluster labels
data['cluster'] = cluster_labels
```

The kmeans.labels_ attribute stores the cluster labels assigned to each data point (customer) in X. We create a new column named "cluster" in the original DataFrame (data) to store these labels. Now, each customer has a corresponding cluster number indicating   their   segment.

Exploring the Results:

With cluster labels assigned, you can analyze the customer segments. Here are some ideas:

- **Visualize the Clusters:** Use data visualization techniques (scatter plots with different colors for clusters) to see how the customer data points are grouped in the feature space.
- **Analyze Cluster Characteristics:** For each cluster, calculate summary statistics of the customer features to understand

what characterizes each segment (e.g., average purchase amount, demographics).

- **Tailored Marketing:** Leverage the insights from the customer segments to develop targeted marketing campaigns and product recommendations for each cluster.

Remember:

This is a basic implementation to get you started. Choosing the optimal n_clusters and interpreting the results effectively often involve further exploration and domain knowledge.

Beyond K-Means:

While K-Means is a powerful tool, there are other unsupervised learning techniques for clustering. As you explore more complex data, consider techniques like hierarchical clustering or density-based clustering, which might be better suited for certain scenarios.

Hands-on Project: Customer Segmentation with K-Means Clustering and Visualization

This project guides you through using K-Means Clustering and Python to segment customers into distinct groups based on their purchase behavior. We'll then visualize the results to gain insights into these customer segments.

Dataset:

For this project, we'll use the publicly available Mall Customer Spending Dataset, which you can download from various online sources (You can search for "Mall_Customers.csv"). This dataset contains information about customer demographics and their spending habits at a shopping mall.

Steps:

1. **Import Libraries and Load Data:**

Python

```python
import pandas as pd
from sklearn.cluster import KMeans
import matplotlib.pyplot as plt

# Load the customer data from the CSV file
(replace 'path/to/data.csv' with your actual file
path)
data = pd.read_csv('path/to/data.csv')
```

We import necessary libraries: pandas for data manipulation, KMeans for clustering, and matplotlib.pyplot for visualization. We then load the customer data into a pandas DataFrame using pd.read_csv. Replace 'path/to/data.csv' with the actual path to your downloaded CSV file.

2. **Preprocess Data**

   Depending on your dataset, you might need to preprocess the data before applying K-Means Clustering. This could involve handling missing values, scaling numerical features, or encoding categorical features (if applicable).

   For this example, we'll assume the data is ready for clustering. However, it's good practice to explore your data and perform any necessary cleaning or transformations before proceeding.

3. **Select Features for Clustering:**

Python

```
# Choose features that best represent customer
spending behavior (e.g., Annual Income, Spending
Score)
X = data[['Annual Income', 'Spending Score']]
```

We create a new DataFrame X containing only the features relevant to customer segmentation in this case, such as 'Annual Income' and 'Spending Score'. These features will be used for clustering the customers.

4. **Define the Number of Clusters (K):**

Python

```
# Experiment with different values of K to
identify the optimal segmentation
n_clusters = 3  # Start with 3 clusters and
experiment with different values
```

This defines the number of customer segments you'd like to create using K-Means. Here, we start with n_clusters=3, but you can experiment with different values to see which one yields the most meaningful   segmentation   for   your   data.

5. **Create and Train the K-Means Model:**

Python

```
# Create a KMeans model with the specified number
of clusters
kmeans = KMeans(n_clusters=n_clusters)

# Train the model on the customer data (X)
kmeans.fit(X)
```

Here, we create a KMeans object specifying the desired number of clusters (n_clusters). Then, we train the model on the prepared customer   data   (X)   using   the   fit   method.

6. **Assign Cluster Labels to Customers:**

Python

```python
# Get the cluster labels for each customer
cluster_labels = kmeans.labels_

# Add a new column to the DataFrame to store the
cluster labels
data['cluster'] = cluster_labels
```

The kmeans.labels_ attribute stores the cluster labels assigned to each customer data point in X. We create a new column named "cluster" in the original DataFrame (data) to store these labels. Now, each customer has a corresponding cluster number indicating their segment.

7. **Visualize the Clusters:**

Python

```python
# Visualize the clusters using a scatter plot with
different colors for each cluster
plt.scatter(X['Annual Income'], X['Spending
Score'], c=cluster_labels)
plt.xlabel('Annual Income')
```

```
plt.ylabel('Spending Score')
plt.title('Customer Segmentation (K-Means)')
plt.show()
```

This code snippet creates a scatter plot using matplotlib. The x-axis represents 'Annual Income', the y-axis represents 'Spending Score', and the color of each data point corresponds to its assigned cluster label (cluster_labels). This visualization helps you see how the customer data points are grouped within the feature space based on their   spending   behavior.

8. **Analyze the Segments (Optional):**

   With cluster labels assigned, you can delve deeper into understanding the customer segments:

   ○ **Segment Characteristics:** For each cluster, calculate summary statistics of the customer features (e.g., average income, average spending score) This will help you understand what characterizes each customer segment, such as high-income, high-spending customers in one cluster, or low-income, budget-conscious customers in another.

9. **Targeted Marketing:** Leverage the insights from the customer segments to develop targeted marketing campaigns and product recommendations. For example, you might offer premium products or exclusive discounts to the high-income segment, while focusing on value deals and budget-friendly options for the low-income segment.

Remember:

- Choosing the optimal n_clusters is an iterative process. Experiment with different values and evaluate the results using visualization techniques or metrics like the Silhouette Coefficient (refer to online resources).
- K-Means assumes spherical clusters. If your data has more complex cluster shapes, other unsupervised learning techniques might be a better fit.

Additional Tips:

- Explore dimensionality reduction techniques like Principal Component Analysis (PCA) if you have many features, as this can help visualize the data in a lower-dimensional space.
- Consider using techniques like hierarchical clustering or density-based clustering for more complex data segmentation scenarios.

This project equips you with the basics of customer segmentation using K-Means Clustering and Python visualization. As you explore more datasets and techniques, you'll gain deeper insights into the hidden patterns within your customer data!

CHAPTER 9: DIMENSIONALITY REDUCTION: MAKING SENSE OF COMPLEX DATA

While navigating a dense forest – the abundance of trees and foliage can make it difficult to see the bigger picture. Similarly, in machine learning, working with high-dimensional data – data with many features – can be overwhelming. The sheer number of features can pose challenges:

- **Curse of Dimensionality:** As the number of features grows, the amount of data needed for training models increases exponentially. This can lead to overfitting, where the model performs well on training data but poorly on unseen data.
- **Increased Computational Cost:** Training models on high-dimensional data requires more computational resources and time.
- **Interpretability Issues:** With many features, it becomes difficult to understand the relative importance of each feature and how they contribute to the model's predictions.

Dimensionality reduction techniques come to the rescue, acting like expert forest guides, helping us navigate the complexity of high-dimensional data. They aim to reduce the number of features while preserving the most important information for analysis and modeling.

9.1 The Power of Principal Component Analysis (PCA)

Have you ever gotten lost in a maze of information overload? In the world of machine learning, high-dimensional data – data with many features – can create a similar challenge. The sheer number of features can make it difficult to analyze, visualize, and even train models effectively.

This is where dimensionality reduction techniques come in, acting like expert navigators through complex data landscapes. One of the most powerful techniques is Principal Component Analysis (PCA). PCA excels at reducing the number of features in your data while preserving the most important information.

Here's a breakdown of how PCA works:

1. **Finding the Underlying Structure:** PCA analyzes the data to identify the hidden patterns and relationships between the existing features. Imagine a cloud of data points representing customers, with features like purchase history and demographics. PCA would find the underlying structure

within this data, revealing how these features connect.

2. **Extracting Principal Components:** Based on the discovered structure, PCA creates a new set of features called principal components (PCs). Think of these PCs as new directions or axes that capture the most significant variations within the data. In our customer example, a PC might represent a "budget-conscious customer" profile, while another might represent a "high-spending" profile.

3. **Dimensionality Reduction:** The key benefit of PCA is that these principal components represent the most important information from the original features. By focusing on a smaller set of PCs (usually the ones explaining most of the data's variance), we can effectively reduce the dimensionality of the data. This is like summarizing the complex customer data into a more manageable set of key factors.

The Analogy: Sailing in Lower Dimensions

Imagine a collection of sailboats scattered across a vast ocean (the high-dimensional data). PCA helps us identify the two most important wind directions (the principal components) that explain how the sailboats move. By focusing on these two wind directions, we can effectively represent the movement of the sailboats in a lower-dimensional space (2 dimensions instead of the original high-dimensional space). This allows us to analyze the sailboat positions and movements more easily.

Benefits of PCA:

- **Reduces Overfitting:** By reducing dimensionality, PCA helps prevent models from overfitting to the training data, leading to better generalization on unseen data.
- **Improves Computational Efficiency:** Working with fewer features translates to faster training times and reduced computational resources needed for models.
- **Enhances Visualization:** PCA allows us to visualize high-dimensional data in lower-dimensional spaces, making it easier to identify patterns and relationships.

In the next section, we'll delve into implementing PCA with Python's scikit-learn library.

9.2 Implementing PCA with Python

PCA offers a powerful tool for navigating the complexities of high-dimensional data. Let's leverage Python's scikit-learn library to see how we can implement PCA for dimensionality reduction:

Scenario: Imagine you work for a company that analyzes customer behavior on a website. You have a dataset with many features, including time spent on different pages, clicks on various elements, and product category preferences. This high dimensionality can make it challenging to analyze user behavior patterns. PCA can help!

Steps:

1. **Import Libraries:**

Python

```python
from sklearn.decomposition import PCA
```

We import PCA from scikit-learn for dimensionality reduction.

2. **Load and Prepare Data:**

Python

```
# Load your customer behavior data (replace
'path/to/data.csv' with your actual file path)
import pandas as pd
data = pd.read_csv('path/to/data.csv')

# Select the features relevant to user behavior
analysis (e.g., time on pages, clicks)
X = data[['feature1', 'feature2', ...]]
```

Here, we load the customer behavior data using pandas and replace 'path/to/data.csv' with the actual path to your data file. Then, we select the features most relevant to user behavior analysis (e.g., time spent on specific pages, clicks on elements) and store them in a DataFrame named X.

3. **Define the Number of Principal Components:**

Python

```
# Define the number of principal components (usually start with explaining a high variance)
n_components = 2  # We'll reduce the data to 2 dimensions for visualization (can be adjusted)
```

This defines the number of principal components (PCs) you want to retain after dimensionality reduction. A common starting point is to choose a number of PCs that explain a high percentage of the variance in the data. Here, we'll use n_components=2 for visualization purposes (you can experiment with different values).

4. **Create and Fit the PCA Model:**

Python

```
# Create a PCA object with the specified number of components
```

```
pca = PCA(n_components=n_components)
```

```
# Fit the PCA model on the data (learn the principal components)
```

```
pca.fit(X)
```

We create a PCA object specifying the desired number of components (n_components). Then, we use the fit method to train (fit) the PCA model on the data (X). This allows the model to learn the underlying structure of the data and identify the most important variations.

5. **Transform the Data:**

Python

Transform the data using the fitted PCA model

X_reduced = pca.transform(X)

The transform method applies the fitted PCA model to the original data (X). The output, stored in X_reduced, represents the data projected onto the most important principal components. In essence, this is the reduced-dimensionality version of your data.

Remember:

- Choosing the optimal number of PCs can be iterative. You can explore the explained variance ratio (refer to pca.explained_variance_ratio_) to understand how much variance each PC captures.
- PCA assumes linear relationships between features. If your data exhibits non-linear relationships, consider alternative dimensionality reduction techniques.

Next Steps:

With the reduced-dimensional data (X_reduced), you can now perform various tasks:

- **Visualization:** Visualize the data points in the lower-dimensional space using techniques like scatter plots to identify patterns in user behavior.
- **Machine Learning:** Use the reduced-dimensional data to train machine learning models that are more efficient and less prone to overfitting due to the lower number of features.

The next section will showcase a hands-on project applying PCA to a real-world dataset and visualizing the results in Python.

9.3 Hands-on Project: PCA in Action

Now that you're equipped with the knowledge of PCA, let's apply it to a real-world scenario and visualize the results in Python!

Scenario: Imagine you're a data analyst for a retail company. You have a dataset containing information about customer purchases, including product category (e.g., clothing, electronics, homeware), purchase amount, and brand. This data is high-dimensional, making it challenging to analyze overall customer purchasing trends. PCA can help!

Steps:

1. Import Libraries and Load Data:

Python

```python
import pandas as pd

from sklearn.decomposition import PCA

import matplotlib.pyplot as plt


# Load your customer purchase data (replace 'path/to/data.csv' with your actual file path)

data = pd.read_csv('path/to/data.csv')
```

We import necessary libraries: pandas for data manipulation, PCA for dimensionality reduction, and matplotlib.pyplot for visualization. Then, we load the customer purchase data into a pandas DataFrame using pd.read_csv. Replace 'path/to/data.csv' with the actual path to your CSV file.

2. **Preprocess Data (Optional):**

   Depending on your dataset, you might need to preprocess the data before applying PCA. This could involve handling missing values, encoding categorical features (if applicable), or scaling numerical features (especially if the features have different units).

   For this example, we'll assume the data is ready for PCA. However, it's good practice to explore your data and perform any necessary cleaning or transformations before proceeding.

3. **Select Features for Analysis:**

Python

```
# Choose features that best represent customer purchase behavior (e.g.,
purchase amount, one-hot encoded product categories)

X = data[['purchase_amount', 'category_electronics', 'category_clothing',
'category_homeware']]
```

We create a new DataFrame X containing the features most relevant to understanding customer purchasing behavior. In this case, we select 'purchase_amount' and one-hot encoded category features ('category_electronics', 'category_clothing', and 'category_homeware'). These features will be used for dimensionality reduction using PCA.

4. **Perform PCA:**

Python

```
# Define the number of principal components (experiment with different
values)
```

n_components = 2 # We'll reduce the data to 2 dimensions for visualization

Create and fit the PCA model

pca = PCA(n_components=n_components)

pca.fit(X)

Transform the data to the reduced-dimensionality space

X_reduced = pca.transform(X)

Here, we define the number of principal components (n_components) we want to retain after dimensionality reduction. We'll use n_components=2 to visualize the data in a two-dimensional space. Then, we create a PCA object specifying the number of components and fit the model on the prepared data (X) using the fit method. Finally, we transform the original data (X) into the lower-dimensional space using the transform method. The output, stored in X_reduced, represents the data projected onto the most important principal   components.

5. **Visualize the Reduced Data:**

Python

```
# Visualize the data points in the first two principal components
plt.scatter(X_reduced[:, 0], X_reduced[:, 1])
plt.xlabel('PC1')
plt.ylabel('PC2')
plt.title('Customer Purchases (PCA)')
plt.show()
```

This code snippet creates a scatter plot using matplotlib. The x-axis represents the first principal component (PC1), and the y-axis represents the second principal component (PC2). Each data point in the scatter plot represents a customer's purchase behavior, projected onto the two most important principal components. By analyzing the positions of the data points, you might identify clusters of customers with similar purchasing patterns. For example, a cluster in the top right corner might represent customers who spend more on electronics, while a cluster in the bottom left might represent budget-conscious customers who tend to purchase homeware items.

Remember:

- Choosing the optimal number of PCs can be iterative. You can explore the explained variance ratio (refer to pca.explained_variance_ratio_) to understand how much variance each PC captures.
- Visualizing the data in lower dimensions helps identify patterns, but it's important to interpret the PCs in the context of the original features to understand what the principal components represent

Part 4:

Putting It All Together

Chapter 10: The Data-Driven Decision-Making Framework

In today's data-rich world, organizations are bombarded with information. But how do you transform this data into actionable insights that drive strategic decisions? This chapter equips you with a practical framework for data-driven decision-making, empowering you to harness the power of data for informed choices.

10.1 Defining the Problem and Setting Objectives

Have you ever felt overwhelmed by a flood of data, unsure where to begin? In the world of data analysis, clearly defining the problem and setting objectives is the compass that guides you towards meaningful insights. Just like any successful journey, a data analysis project thrives on a well-defined destination.

Here's a breakdown of this crucial first step:

1. Identifying the Business Challenge:

The starting point is understanding the specific business problem you're trying to solve. Is it a marketing campaign that's underperforming, a rise in customer complaints, or difficulty predicting inventory needs? Clearly articulating the challenge ensures your data analysis efforts are targeted and relevant.

Example: Imagine you work for a company that provides online streaming services. You've noticed a recent dip in user engagement, with fewer users actively watching content on the platform. This is your business challenge.

2. Establishing SMART Objectives:

Once you've identified the problem, it's time to set specific, measurable, achievable, relevant, and time-bound (SMART) objectives for your analysis. These objectives will be the roadmap guiding your data exploration and model selection.

- **Specific:** What exactly do you want to achieve with the data analysis? Vague goals like "improve user engagement" won't provide enough direction. Instead, aim for a more specific objective like "increase the average daily watch time per user by 10% within the next quarter."
- **Measurable:** How will you track progress towards your objective? Define metrics that quantify success. In our example, "average daily watch time" is a measurable metric.

- **Achievable:** Be ambitious, but also realistic. Ensure your objectives are achievable within the given timeframe and resource constraints.
- **Relevant:** The objectives should directly address the business challenge you identified. Don't get sidetracked by analyzing data that doesn't contribute to solving the core problem.
- **Time-bound:** Set a deadline for achieving your objectives. This timeframe keeps the project focused and ensures progress is being made.

Following the SMART framework keeps your data analysis project on track and focused on delivering real business value.

By clearly defining the problem and setting SMART objectives, you lay the foundation for a successful data analysis journey. In the next section, we'll delve into the crucial step of data preparation, where we get our data ready for analysis!

10.2 Feature Engineering and Data Preparation

Imagine you're a chef preparing a delicious meal. You wouldn't throw unwashed vegetables and random ingredients into a pot and expect a culinary masterpiece. Similarly, in data analysis, raw data needs careful preparation before it can be used to create insightful models. This is where feature engineering and data preparation come into play.

Think of data preparation as cleaning and organizing your ingredients, while feature engineering is like chopping, dicing, and potentially even mixing ingredients to create something new and more useful for your recipe (model).

Let's explore these key steps:

1. Data Cleaning and Preprocessing:

Real-world data is rarely perfect. It might contain missing values, inconsistencies, and formatting errors. Data cleaning and preprocessing address these issues to ensure the data is consistent and usable for analysis. Here are some common techniques:

- **Handling Missing Values:** Missing data points can be imputed (filled in) using various techniques like mean/median imputation or more sophisticated methods. The choice of imputation method depends on the data and the specific missing value pattern.
- **Outlier Handling:** Outliers are data points that fall far outside the expected range. They can be addressed by

winsorization (capping outliers to a certain threshold) or removal if they are truly erroneous.

- **Data Type Conversion:** Ensure features have consistent data types (e.g., numerical or categorical) appropriate for the analysis and chosen models.

Code Example (using pandas for basic data cleaning):

Python

```python
import pandas as pd




# Load your data (replace 'path/to/data.csv' with your actual file path)

data = pd.read_csv('path/to/data.csv')




# Check for missing values

print(data.isnull().sum())   # This shows the count of missing values in each feature
```

Impute missing numerical values with the mean (replace with other methods if needed)

```python
data['numerical_feature'] = data['numerical_feature'].fillna(data['numerical_feature'].mean())
```

Encode categorical features using one-hot encoding (replace with other methods if needed)

```python
data = pd.get_dummies(data, columns=['categorical_feature'])
```

2. Feature Engineering:

Existing features in your data might not be directly usable in machine learning models. Feature engineering involves creating new features from existing ones or transforming features to improve model performance. Here are some common techniques:

- **Feature Creation:** Combine existing features (e.g., ratio of two features) or create new features based on domain knowledge to capture relevant information. For example, you might create a new feature "time since last purchase" from a customer dataset.
- **Feature Scaling:** Features with different scales can affect model performance. Techniques like standardization (scaling to zero mean and unit variance) or normalization (scaling to a specific range) can address this.
- **Dimensionality Reduction:** If you have a high number of features, dimensionality reduction techniques like Principal Component Analysis (PCA) can help reduce the number of features while preserving most of the information.

Remember: Feature engineering is an iterative process. Explore different techniques and evaluate their impact on model performance.

3. Exploratory Data Analysis (EDA):

Before diving into complex models, get to know your data! Exploratory Data Analysis (EDA) involves techniques like visualization (histograms, scatter plots) and summary statistics to understand:

- **Data Distribution:** How are the features distributed (e.g., normal, skewed)?
- **Relationships between Features:** Are there any correlations between features that might be relevant for your analysis?
- **Patterns and Trends:** Can you identify any underlying patterns or trends in the data that could inform your modeling strategy?

By investing time in data preparation and feature engineering, you ensure your models are built on a solid foundation and have a higher chance of success.

The next section will delve into model selection and evaluation, where you choose the right tool (model) for the job based on your prepared data!

10.3 Model Selection and Evaluation: Choosing the Right Tool for the Job

You've meticulously cleaned and prepared your data, and now it's time to unleash its potential! This section dives into model selection and evaluation, the crucial step where you choose the most suitable machine learning model for your specific problem.

Think of models as tools in a toolbox. A hammer is great for driving nails, but not so effective for sawing wood. Similarly, different models excel at different tasks. Here's how to make an informed decision:

1. Understanding Model Types:

There's no one-size-fits-all model. The best choice depends on the nature of your problem and the type of predictions you want to make:

- **Classification:** If you're trying to predict a category (e.g., customer churn – churn or not churn, spam email – spam or not spam), classification models like decision trees, random forests, or support vector machines (SVMs) are strong contenders.
- **Regression:** For continuous predictions (e.g., sales forecast, housing price prediction), regression models like linear regression, ridge regression, or lasso regression are well-suited.
- **Clustering:** If your goal is to group similar data points together (e.g., customer segmentation), unsupervised learning

techniques like k-means clustering or hierarchical clustering can be valuable.

2. Model Training and Evaluation:

Once you've chosen a model type based on your problem, it's time to train it on your data. Here's a breakdown of the process:

- **Training-Testing Split:** Split your data into two sets: a training set used to train the model and a testing set used to evaluate its performance on unseen data. This helps prevent overfitting, where the model performs well on the training data but poorly on new data.
- **Model Training:** The training process involves feeding the training data to the chosen model. The model learns patterns and relationships within the data to make predictions.
- **Model Evaluation:** Use the testing set to evaluate the model's performance. Common metrics include accuracy (for classification) or mean squared error (MSE) (for regression). These metrics tell you how well the model's predictions generalize to unseen data.

Code Example (using scikit-learn for basic training/testing split and model evaluation):

Python

```python
from sklearn.model_selection import train_test_split
from sklearn.metrics import accuracy_score

# Load your prepared data (replace with your data loading code)
X = ...  # Your features
y = ...  # Your target variable

# Split data into training and testing sets (70% for training, 30% for testing)
X_train, X_test, y_train, y_test = train_test_split(X, y, test_size=0.3, random_state=42)

# Train a model (replace with your chosen model)
from sklearn.ensemble import RandomForestClassifier
model = RandomForestClassifier()
model.fit(X_train, y_train)

# Make predictions on the testing set
y_pred = model.predict(X_test)
```

```
# Evaluate model performance (accuracy in this case)
accuracy = accuracy_score(y_test, y_pred)
print("Model Accuracy:", accuracy)
```

3. Model Tuning and Hyperparameter Optimization:

Most models have parameters that can be adjusted to improve performance. These parameters are called hyperparameters. Hyperparameter tuning involves trying different combinations of hyperparameter values and evaluating the model's performance on a validation set (a separate set from the training and testing sets) to find the optimal configuration.

Remember: Model selection and evaluation is an iterative process. Experiment with different models, evaluate their performance, and refine your approach based on the results.

The next section will guide you through building a comprehensive data analysis workflow, putting all the pieces together for a real-world scenario!

10.4 Hands-on Project: Building a Data Analysis Workflow

Now that you're equipped with the essential knowledge of data-driven decision making, let's get hands-on! This project will guide you through developing a comprehensive data analysis workflow for a chosen business problem, utilizing Python libraries.

Scenario: Imagine you're a data analyst for a retail company. You're tasked with building a model to predict customer churn (the likelihood of a customer stopping business) to develop targeted customer retention strategies. Here's a step-by-step approach:

Step 1: Problem Definition and Objectives

- **Problem Definition:** Clearly define the problem as predicting customer churn.
- **Objective:** Develop a machine learning model to identify customers at high risk of churn with an accuracy of at least 80%.

Step 2: Data Acquisition and Exploration

1. **Data Acquisition:** Obtain customer data from relevant sources within the company, potentially including:

- Customer demographics (age, location, income)
- Purchase history (frequency, amount, product categories)
- Interactions with the company (website visits, support tickets)

2. **Exploratory Data Analysis (EDA):**

- Use pandas library to load and explore the data:

Python

```
import pandas as pd
```

```
# Load customer data (replace 'path/to/data.csv' with your actual file path)
```

```
data = pd.read_csv('path/to/data.csv')
```

Analyze customer demographics and purchase behavior to understand churn patterns.

Visualize the data using techniques like histograms (distribution of purchase frequency) and boxplots (comparing purchase amounts across different customer segments).

Step 3: Data Preprocessing

1. **Handle Missing Values:** Identify missing values and employ appropriate imputation techniques (e.g., mean/median imputation) to fill in missing entries.

2. **Encode Categorical Features:** If your data contains categorical features (e.g., customer location), encode them using techniques like one-hot encoding (suitable for scikit-learn models) to prepare them for modeling.

3. **Feature Engineering (Optional):**

   ○ Create new features that might be relevant for churn prediction. For instance, calculate customer lifetime value (total spending) or purchase frequency (number of purchases per unit time).
   ○ Consider feature scaling techniques (e.g., standardization) if features have different ranges to improve model performance.

Step 4: Model Selection and Training

1. **Choose a Model:** Since customer churn is a classification problem (churn or not churn), suitable models include decision trees, random forests, or support vector machines (SVMs). We'll use a Random Forest Classifier here due to its interpretability and robustness to overfitting.

2. **Train-Test Split:** Split your prepared data into training and testing sets using scikit-learn's train_test_split function. The training set will be used to train the model, and the testing set will be used to evaluate its performance on unseen data.

3. **Model Training:** Train the chosen model (Random Forest Classifier in this case) on the training set using the fit method.

4. **Model Evaluation:** Make predictions on the testing set using the predict method and evaluate the model's performance using a metric like accuracy score (percentage of correct predictions).

Code Example (incorporating Steps 2-4):

Python

```python
# Exploratory Data Analysis (replace with your specific code)
# ... (data visualization and analysis steps)


# Data Preprocessing
# Handle missing values (replace with most suitable imputation technique)
data['missing_feature'] = data['missing_feature'].fillna(data['missing_feature'].mean())


# Encode categorical features (replace with appropriate encoding if needed)
data = pd.get_dummies(data, columns=['categorical_feature'])


# Feature Engineering (optional)
# ... (create new features based on your analysis)


# Model Selection and Training
from sklearn.model_selection import train_test_split
from sklearn.ensemble import RandomForestClassifier
from sklearn.metrics import accuracy_score
```

```
# Split data into training and testing sets (70% for training, 30% for testing)
X_train, X_test, y_train, y_test = train_test_split(X, y, test_size=0.3, random_state=42)


# Train the Random Forest Classifier model
model = RandomForestClassifier()
model.fit(X_train, y_train)


# Make predictions on the testing set
y_pred = model.predict(X_test)


# Evaluate model accuracy
accuracy = accuracy_score(y_test, y_pred
```

Step 5: Model Tuning and Improvement (Optional):

While the Random Forest Classifier might provide a good baseline, you can explore further improvement through hyperparameter tuning. Here's a basic approach:

1. **Identify Hyperparameters:** Random Forest has hyperparameters like n_estimators (number of trees) and max_depth (maximum depth of individual trees) that can influence   performance.

2. **Grid Search:** Utilize techniques like GridSearchCV from scikit-learn   to   evaluate   different   combinations   of hyperparameter values and select the configuration that yields the best performance on a validation set (a separate set split from   the   training   data).

Step 6: Deployment and Monitoring

1. **Model Deployment:** If the model achieves the desired accuracy (at least 80% in our case), consider deploying it into a production environment. This could involve integrating the model into the company's systems to identify customers at risk of   churn   in   real-time.

2. **Model Monitoring:** Regularly monitor the model's performance over time. As customer behavior and market trends evolve, the model's accuracy might degrade. Retrain and update the model periodically to maintain its effectiveness.

Remember: This is a simplified example, and the specific steps involved in a data analysis workflow can vary depending on the nature of the problem and the available data. However, it provides a foundational framework to get you started!

By following these steps and leveraging Python libraries like pandas and scikit-learn, you can develop data analysis workflows that empower data-driven decision making within your organization.

Bonus Tip: Explore other machine learning models and feature engineering techniques to potentially improve your model's performance. There's no single "best" approach, and experimentation is key to optimizing your data analysis workflow!

Chapter 11: Communicating Your Insights Effectively

So, you've delved into the data, unearthed valuable insights, and built a powerful model. But your work isn't finished yet! Effectively communicating your findings is crucial for translating data into actionable decisions. This chapter equips you with the skills to become a data storytelling ninja.

11.1 Data Visualization Techniques: Transforming Numbers into Insights

Data analysis is like cracking a code – you unlock hidden patterns and trends. But how do you translate these insights into a language everyone understands? Data visualization comes to the rescue! It's the art of transforming raw numbers into clear, compelling visuals that tell a story.

Here's a breakdown of some essential data visualization techniques you can wield:

1. Bar Charts:

Bar charts are champions for comparing categories or showcasing trends over time. Imagine you're analyzing customer satisfaction ratings for different product categories. A bar chart lets you visualize which category receives the highest (or lowest) ratings.

Code Example (using Matplotlib):

Python

```python
import matplotlib.pyplot as plt


# Sample data (replace with your data)

product_categories = ['Product A', 'Product B', 'Product C']

satisfaction_ratings = [4.2, 3.8, 4.8]


# Create the bar chart

plt.figure(figsize=(8, 6))  # Adjust figure size as needed

plt.bar(product_categories, satisfaction_ratings, color=['skyblue', 'lightcoral', 'lightgreen'])

plt.xlabel('Product Category')

plt.ylabel('Average Satisfaction Rating')

plt.title('Customer Satisfaction by Product Category')
```

```python
plt.xticks(rotation=45) # Rotate x-axis labels for readability if needed
```

```python
plt.grid(axis='y', linestyle='--', alpha=0.7)  # Add subtle gridlines for better readability
```

```python
plt.tight_layout()
```

```python
plt.show()
```

2. Line Charts:

Line charts excel at depicting continuous data trends. Perhaps you're tracking website traffic over the past year. A line chart allows you to visualize these traffic fluctuations, helping identify seasonal trends or marketing campaign impacts.

Code Example (using Matplotlib):

Python

```python
# Sample data (replace with your data)

months = ['Jan', 'Feb', 'Mar', 'Apr', 'May', 'Jun']

website_traffic = [10000, 12000, 15000, 18000, 16000, 14000]
```

```
# Create the line chart

plt.figure(figsize=(8, 6))

plt.plot(months, website_traffic, marker='o', linestyle='-', color='royalblue')

plt.xlabel('Month')

plt.ylabel('Website Traffic')

plt.title('Website Traffic Trends (Past 6 Months)')

plt.xticks(rotation=15)  # Rotate x-axis labels for readability if needed

plt.grid(True)

plt.tight_layout()

plt.show()
```

3. Scatter Plots:

Scatter plots reveal relationships (or lack thereof) between two variables. Imagine you're investigating the correlation between advertising spending and website conversion rates. A scatter plot can visually depict this relationship, helping you identify potential trends.

Code Example (using Matplotlib):

Python

```python
# Sample data (replace with your data)

advertising_spend = [1000, 2000, 3000, 4000, 5000]

conversion_rate = [2, 4, 5, 6, 7]


# Create the scatter plot

plt.figure(figsize=(8, 6))

plt.scatter(advertising_spend, conversion_rate, color='darkorange')

plt.xlabel('Advertising Spend')

plt.ylabel('Website Conversion Rate (%)')

plt.title('Relationship Between Advertising Spend and Conversion Rate')

plt.grid(True)
```

```
plt.tight_layout()

plt.show()
```

These are just a few basic examples. There's a vast world of data visualization techniques waiting to be explored! As you delve deeper, consider incorporating elements like color, size, and interactivity to enhance your visualizations and make them even more impactful.

The next section dives into the art of storytelling with data, where you'll learn how to craft compelling narratives around your data insights.

11.2 Storytelling with Data: Presenting Insights for Informed Decision-Making

Data analysis is like a detective story – you meticulously gather clues, analyze evidence, and finally unveil the truth. But what good is a detective who keeps their findings to themselves? The power of data lies in its ability to inform and influence decisions. Here's where storytelling with data comes in – it's the art of transforming your insights into a captivating narrative that resonates with your audience.

Think of your presentation as a journey you take your audience on. Here are some key steps to ensure they're engaged and ready to act upon your findings:

1. Start with a Clear Context:

Imagine you're a data analyst for a clothing retailer. Set the stage by establishing the business problem – declining sales in a particular clothing category. Briefly explain the objectives of your analysis, like identifying factors contributing to this decline.

2. Focus on Key Insights:

Don't overwhelm your audience with every detail unearthed from the data. Highlight the most impactful findings. Perhaps your analysis revealed a shift in customer demographics or a rise in competition offering similar products.

3. Leverage Data Visualization Effectively:

Data visualizations are the superheroes of storytelling. Integrate impactful charts or graphs that support your narrative. Don't just show visuals – explain them clearly, ensuring your audience understands the key takeaways.

Code Example (incorporating Matplotlib visualization from previous section):

Python

```
# Imagine this chart is included in your presentation to visualize

website traffic trends

plt.figure(figsize=(8, 6))

# ... (plot your website traffic data here)

# ... (add labels, title, etc.)

plt.show()



# During your presentation, you might say:
```

"As you can see from this chart, website traffic has declined slightly over the past few months. This could be a contributing factor to the decrease in sales we're observing in category X."

4. End with Actionable Recommendations:

So what now? The goal is to translate your insights into practical steps the business can take. Based on your findings, recommend potential solutions – maybe it's revamping marketing strategies for category X or exploring new product offerings.

Storytelling with data is a powerful tool that empowers you to connect with your audience on an emotional level and inspire them to take action. By following these steps and practicing your data storytelling skills, you become a persuasive advocate for data-driven decision making within your organization.

Data presentations don't have to be dry and technical. Infuse your narrative with enthusiasm, use anecdotes or analogies to explain complex concepts, and most importantly, tailor your message to your audience's needs and interests.

The next section explores the crucial aspect of ethical considerations in data analysis, ensuring your data storytelling practices are responsible and trustworthy.

11.3 Ethical Considerations in Data Analysis and Responsible Data Use

Data analysis is a powerful tool, but with great power comes great responsibility. As you embark on your data storytelling journey, it's vital to consider the ethical implications of your work. Here are some key principles to keep in mind:

1. Data Privacy:

Data privacy is paramount. Ensure you're using data responsibly and ethically. Here are some questions to ask yourself:

- Do I have proper authorization to use this data?
- Am I anonymizing the data when necessary?
- Am I complying with relevant data privacy regulations (e.g., GDPR)?

Code Example (illustrative, not functional code):

Python

```python
# Imagine you're anonymizing customer data before analysis (replace with your specific anonymization techniques)

def anonymize_data(data):

 # Replace customer names with random IDs

 data['customer_name'] = data['customer_name'].apply(lambda x: str(uuid.uuid4()))

 # ... (apply similar techniques for other sensitive data)

 return data
```

2. Bias Awareness:

Be mindful of potential biases that might creep into your analysis. Biases can stem from the data itself (e.g., sampling bias) or from your own assumptions. Here's how to mitigate them:

- Scrutinize your data sources for potential biases.
- Challenge your own assumptions and consider alternative perspectives.
- Be transparent about limitations and potential biases in your analysis.

3. Transparency:

Transparency builds trust in your data analysis and storytelling. Here are some ways to be transparent:

- Clearly explain your data sources and methodologies.
- Acknowledge limitations of the data and analysis.
- Avoid overstating the certainty of your conclusions.

By upholding ethical principles, you ensure that your data analysis contributes to positive outcomes and builds trust in the power of data-driven decision making.

Remember: Ethical data analysis is not just about following rules – it's about using data for good. By being mindful of these considerations, you become a responsible data storyteller who fosters trust and empowers informed decision-making within your organization.

Appendix: Python Resources and Cheat Sheets

Python is a versatile and powerful programming language widely used in data analysis and machine learning. Here's a curated list of resources to enhance your Python journey:

Official Resources:

- **Python Documentation:** The official Python documentation is an excellent starting point for beginners and experienced programmers alike. It provides comprehensive explanations of Python syntax, libraries, and best practices: https://docs.python.org/
- **Python Tutorial:** This interactive tutorial from the Python website guides you through the basics of Python programming in a step-by-step manner: https://docs.python.org/3/tutorial/

Online Learning Platforms:

- **DataCamp:** DataCamp offers interactive courses and coding challenges specifically geared towards data science and machine learning using Python. They provide a free plan with limited access and paid plans for comprehensive learning: https://www.datacamp.com/

- **Coursera:** Coursera features a wide range of Python programming courses from top universities and institutions. Some courses are free, while others require enrollment: https://www.coursera.org/
- **Udacity:** Udacity offers Nanodegree programs and other learning resources focused on data science and related fields, with Python as a core language: https://www.udacity.com/

Cheat Sheets:

- **Real Python Cheat Sheet:** This cheat sheet from Real Python provides a quick reference for various Python concepts, libraries, and functionalities: https://static.realpython.com/python-cheat-sheet.pdf
- **DataCamp Cheat Sheet:** DataCamp offers downloadable cheat sheets for Python basics, data manipulation with pandas, data visualization with Matplotlib, and more: https://www.datacamp.com/cheat-sheet
- **GeeksforGeeks Python Cheat Sheet:** This cheat sheet from GeeksforGeeks offers a concise overview of Python syntax, operators, data structures, and object-oriented programming concepts: https://www.geeksforgeeks.org/python-cheat-sheet/

Remember: These resources are just a starting point. As you delve deeper into Python and data analysis, you'll discover a vast online community of developers and data enthusiasts willing to share knowledge and answer your questions.

Bonus Tip: Don't be afraid to experiment with code! The best way to learn Python is by getting hands-on and practicing what you learn. There are many online coding playgrounds and platforms where you can write and execute Python code without needing to install software: https://www.onlinegdb.com/online_python_compiler

By utilizing these resources and practicing consistently, you'll develop your Python skills and become a data analysis powerhouse!

Glossary of Statistical Learning Terms

This glossary provides definitions for some key statistical learning terms encountered throughout this book:

- **Algorithm:** A set of step-by-step instructions for solving a problem or performing a task. In machine learning, algorithms learn from data to make predictions or classifications.
- **Bias:** The systematic difference between the predicted values from a model and the actual values. A biased model consistently overestimates or underestimates the true values.
- **Classification:** A machine learning task where the goal is to predict the category (class) an unseen data point belongs to. Examples include classifying emails as spam or not spam, or classifying customer churn (likely to churn or not churn).
- **Data Preprocessing:** The process of cleaning, transforming, and preparing data for analysis. It may involve handling missing values, encoding categorical features, and feature scaling.
- **Evaluation Metrics:** Measures used to assess the performance of a machine learning model on unseen data. Common metrics include accuracy (for classification) or mean squared error (MSE) (for regression).

- **Feature Engineering:** The process of creating new features from existing data that might be more relevant for the machine learning task.

- **Hyperparameter:** A parameter of a machine learning algorithm that is not directly learned from the data but needs to be set before training. Examples include the number of trees in a Random Forest or the learning rate in a linear regression model.

- **Machine Learning:** A subfield of Artificial Intelligence (AI) where algorithms learn from data to make predictions or classifications without being explicitly programmed.

- **Model Selection:** The process of choosing the most suitable machine learning model for a specific problem based on the nature of the data and the desired outcome.

- **Overfitting:** A phenomenon where a model performs well on the training data but poorly on unseen data. It occurs when the model learns the noise or specific details in the training data instead of capturing the underlying general patterns.

- **Regression:** A machine learning task where the goal is to predict a continuous numerical value, such as sales figures or housing prices.

- **Supervised Learning:** A machine learning paradigm where the training data includes both input features and the desired output values (labels). The model learns the relationship between the features and labels to make predictions for unseen data.

- **Unsupervised Learning:** A machine learning paradigm where the training data consists only of input features, and the goal is to uncover hidden patterns or structures within the data. Clustering is a common type of unsupervised learning task.

This glossary covers some of the essential terms encountered in the book. As you delve deeper into data analysis and machine learning, you'll encounter a wider range of terminology. Don't hesitate to consult online resources or other reference materials to expand your statistical learning vocabulary!

www.ingramcontent.com/pod-product-compliance
Lightning Source LLC
LaVergne TN
LVHW081522050326
832903LV00025B/1582